LONDON TREE WALKS

Paul Wood is the author of *London's Street Trees* (also in Safe Haven Books), now in its second, completely revised edition, and *London is a Forest*, and the editor of the *Great Trees of London Map*. He photographs and writes about trees and urban nature on *thestreettree.com*, and leads London tree walks around the capital regularly. Follow him on social media as *@TheStreetTree*. He lives in well-forested Islington.

LONDON TREE WALKS

Arboreal Ambles through the Green Metropolis

PAUL WOOD

SAFE HAVEN

For my parents

First published 2020 by Safe Haven Books Ltd
12 Chinnocks Wharf
14 Narrow Street
London E14 8DJ
www.safehavenbooks.co.uk

ISBN 978 1 9160453 4 7

10 9 8 7 6 5 4 3 2 1

The Safe Haven team on *London's Tree Walks*: Paul Wood, Graham
Coster, Caroline Atkins, Caroline Buckland, David Welch

Designed by paulwoodcreative.co.uk
Set in Gill Sans and Tablet Gothic SemiCondensed

Printed and bound in the EU by Graphy Cems

*Take care to cross roads using designated crossings. Please be
mindful that trees on private property may be viewed only from
the street, and respect people's privacy.*

Right: Accumulator Tower, Churchill Gardens
Page 1: Parkland Walk
Page 2-3: Photinia 'Red Robin' at Crofton Park

Acknowledgements

I am indebted to many people who have helped bring this book to fruition, by pounding the pavements, sharing their wisdom and identifying difficult trees. Some of these elude me still, and I will be very grateful for any definitive identifications (or indeed, corrections).

Thanks go to these people:

Caroline Atkins
Sara Bishop
Caroline Buckland
Peter Coles
John Crompton
Angela Forrester
Mark Johnston

Sean Harkin
Richard Marmalade
Xanthe Mosley
Clodagh O'Neill
Greg Packman
Katherine Pogson
Andrew Stuck

My special thanks to Graham Coster for devising the Rock Family Trees walk and for his invaluable musical and general knowledge.

Picture credits

All photos © Paul Wood, except:
21   Nick Catford, disused-stations.org.uk
23   Mark Johnston
64   Artokoloro/Alamy
75, 85, 91, 112, 117, 121, 127, 148, 149, 156   Graham Coster
76   Danny McL
84   © Museum of London
87   Mary Evans
88   © PLA Collection/Museum of London
96, 106   © Southwark Local History Library and Archive
97   London School of Economics
132   Arcaid Images/Alamy
140   Henk Snoek / RIBA Collections
159   Philip Townsend, Camera Press, London
160   Evening Standard/Hulton Archive/Getty Images
161   © Sheila Rock
166   © Adrian Boot/urbanimage.tv
182   Heritage Images Partnership/Alamy
190   Hilary Morgan/Alamy
200   iStock
210   History in Pictures
216   © Christie's Images/Bridgeman Images

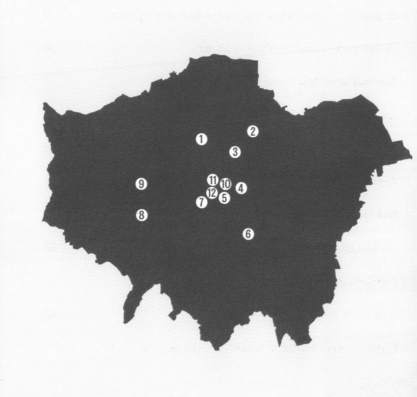

Contents

Introduction

How do you set about publicising a book called *London's Street Trees*? Back in 2017, when my first book came out, no-one had ever published anything like it. So my publisher and I came up with the idea of adapting the usual convention of the bookshop signing.

Find a shop in a suitably leafy neighbourhood, and offer a guided walk from the front door, to point out the remarkable variety of trees to be found on the surrounding streets, before delivering the amazed customers back to the shop for, of course, the grateful purchase of their signed copy. Village Books in Dulwich Village signed up straight away, sold out almost as quickly, and suddenly the 'tree walk' had been invented.

It is not an exaggeration to say I have been busy ever since. Other bookshops followed, and I soon realised, pretty much anywhere in London is suitable for a tree walk. Over the last three years I have been leading regular 'Explorations of the Urban Forest' with the Museum of Walking, some of the routes included in this book have their genesis in those tours.

Invitations to lead groups around urban trees have come in from Shoreditch, Brockley, Chiswick and elsewhere; I have found myself doing tree walks in Sheffield, Dublin and even Philadelphia.

Why have they been so popular? Partly it is that, in London in the twenty-first century, we are in a golden age of civic tree planting: within five minutes' walk of Hackney's Broadway Market you can be showing people some pretty exotic species, from Peanut Butter Trees to Bee-bee Trees – just planted in the street. But also, I discovered, the clientele for my tree walks were not merely local: people were travelling considerable distances to take part. It wasn't just the chance to be taken somewhere you hadn't been before: this universe of trees was itself somewhere people hadn't been, where literally every corner holds the possibility of a new and thrilling discovery.

At the back of *London's Street Trees* we had decided to include four very short walking routes, to let readers go on their own expeditions of discovery. As the first edition went into its first, then second, then third reprint I realised that these Tree Walks were one of the most popular features in the book. So in the new, expanded 2020 edition

London Fields

we added two more. When lockdown hit just as it was published, and no more than an hour's daily exercise outside was permitted, what was the only encounter with the natural world available to most Londoners? Their neighbourhood trees.

So why not do a whole book of tree walks? Here we are, then: twelve longer – in some cases much longer – tree walks, this time taking in not just the capital's street trees but its glorious abundance of parks, squares and gardens, and spread out across all points of the compass. They will take you to parts of Greater London you've never been before – but also to see parts you think you already know in a new light.

As well as offering a superb variety of arboreal facts, anecdotes and species from start to finish, each walk follows a theme. In south-west London we follow a musical trail from Marc Bolan to Bob Marley;

in Bermondsey we celebrate pioneering mayor Ada Salter's dedication to beautifying her far-from-prosperous borough, not least with some determined tree-planting; Ealing sees the quixotic search for an elephant supposedly interred under an oak tree. We go back in time tracing the trees that have made their mark on London for centuries, and we end our walk through London's Docklands amid the still-under-construction twenty-first century.

But while these tree walks will show you a multiplicity of species you probably never thought to find in London – Persian Silk Trees, Giant Redwoods, Manchurian Walnuts – we haven't mentioned the one arboreal landmark along every single walk in this book.

The London Plane may actually only make up 3% of the capital's tree population, but it is the tree by which you will know you are in London. It was the first species planted to monumentalise the city, the first to line our streets in numbers, with the building of the Embankment. Go in search of trees like this – many still magnificently and toweringly alive – and you are looking at how London itself has grown.

But think, as you take these walks: what would a Londoner of the future find, in 50 or 100 years, on these routes? Will climate change mean that they'll be walking down avenues of purple-blazing Jacarandas, like in Lisbon or Buenos Aires? Will some of our commercial districts and shopping malls be abandoned to the Tree of Heaven and the Sycamore? Or will London be even more of a world city, of trees and people, than it is already?

Lapsed Hornbeam coppice, Coldfall Wood

North London's Ancient Woodland

A Highgate Circular

We start this book among some of London's oldest
tree cover: precious remnants of the ancient woodland that
was here before the city itself. This is how London looked
before it was London. Despite being just a few miles
from the centre of London, most of the route is through
remarkably tranquil green spaces, and also takes you through
some newer woods and along streets that now cover
what would once have been woodland. It's quite long,
but there's an option to make it shorter.
Part of it follows a section of the Capital Ring, one of
London's long-distance footpaths. But there are decidedly
urban sections too: the Edwardian grandeur of Muswell
Hill can be contrasted with some of the interwar
streets of Fortis Green and the artisan terraces of
East Finchley, as well as a glimpse of some of
Highgate's desirable neighbourhoods.

Length: 7 miles (15,000 steps)
Start and Finish: Highgate Tube station (Northern Line)
Shortening: East Finchley Tube station (Northern Line)
Accessibility: unmade paths, steps, and steep slopes
Relative Difficulty: 4/5

1 – Priory Gardens and Queen's Wood

Leave Highgate Tube station via the Priory Gardens exit and head straight ahead down this leafy suburban street lined with 1930s Tudorbethan semis. Several front gardens hold impressive trees including a **Lawson's Cypress** and a magnificent **Sycamore** or two. But beyond the rooftops a thick woodland canopy beckons: this is Queen's Wood.

After 200 metres, just beyond a mature **Whitebeam** street tree, and as the road begins to curve to the right, turn left on the concrete path signposted as both the Capital Ring and 'Footpath Through Queen's Wood'. This curves gently down past several more large **Sycamores** and into the wood.

Arriving in a well-worn hollow, you'll see sycamores give way to towering mature **Oaks** and **Hornbeams** with a dense shrubby understorey of **Holly**, **Hawthorn** and, very sparsely, **Wild Service Tree**. Several routes diverge from here, but we stick to the Capital Ring and head straight up the wide, stepped path ahead and slightly to the left.

Along the way, notice how the leaves of different oak trees differ. There are two different species of oak in the woods, or three if you count hybrids: the Pedunculate or English Oak and Sessile Oak. They are quite similar, but sessile oaks (the less frequent species) have leaves with a distinct stem or petiole connecting it to the branch; pedunculate oaks, on the other hand, have no petiole. This feature is reversed in the species' acorns: sessile oaks produce stalk-less (or sessile) acorns, while pedunculate oaks have acorns with stalks (or peduncles). These two species will hybridise readily and produce a tree known, botanically, as *Quercus x rosaceae*, with characteristics midway between the two species.

After 400 metres, the path emerges onto Queen's Wood Road, a thoroughfare cutting off the southern section of the wood from its main northern section. It was constructed in 1900 and became a through road connecting to Wood Vale in 1930. Look out for traffic as you cross the road and continue along the main Capital Ring path. After about 300 metres, we divert from the Capital Ring by taking a right fork just after a bench and before a dead standing tree. This leads steeply downhill to Frog Pond. Frog Pond is fed by a frequently dry stream, one

Whitebeam on Priory Gardens

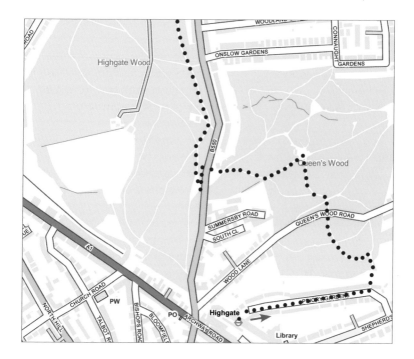

of two sources of the River Moselle that rise in the wood. North London's Moselle should not be confused with the major continental river of the same name: this is a tributary of Pymmes Brook, itself a tributary of the River Lea. Beyond the woods, it runs mostly below ground, appearing briefly at Lordship Recreation Ground and Tottenham Cemetery.

Frog Pond is a good point from which to survey the geography of the wood. Its marked undulations are, in a small way, rather dramatic, and another indication of the wood's ancient status – contours unlevelled by modern machinery. From here we head 'upstream' by the Moselle along a tarmacked path to rejoin the Capital Ring, noting an avenue of **London Planes** planted either side. As they merge into the

wood, it is the planes' striking bark that sets them apart from the more usual oaks and hornbeams. Perhaps they date back to 1898, when the wood took the name Queen's Wood and planting planes all over London

Capital Ring signposts

Wood anemones

you are crossing a wood bank, an ancient feature that would once have marked the wood's edge. This low mound is thought to have been dug in the late sixteenth century, and would once have been lined with pollarded boundary-marking trees and deadwood hedging, which it has recently been embellished with once again. Continue in a straight line up the slope and take a minor detour through the railings to admire a particularly dramatic **Hornbeam** that may well be a surviving boundary tree. Gnarled and tortured, it has clearly been pollarded in the distant past.

was *de rigueur*. Unlike the more typical flaking bark with its mottled camouflage pattern, on these trees the burry, corky boles are a characteristic associated with the **'Pyramidalis'** cultivar.

Where the paths meet, old iron fencing and an interpretation board announce that

Rejoining the path, follow it uphill to the very good Queen's Wood Café, housed in a striking Edwardian building complete with turret and shady verandah surrounded by an organic garden. Leave the wood by a gate next to it and emerge on busy Muswell Hill Road.

Queen's Wood Café

Queen's Wood

Queen's Wood was so named in 1898 in honour of Queen Victoria, prior to which it was known as Churchyard Bottom Wood, a descriptive local name likely to have arisen over many centuries. It is an ancient wood, and has some of the typical flora associated with very old woodlands including extensive patches of white-flowering wood anemone, best seen in March.

Historically, it would have been a wood of oak standards (single trunked trees left to grow tall and straight for many decades) and hornbeam coppice (a thicket of thin stems arising from a 'stool' and cut back every few years) but, not having been coppiced for over a hundred years, and probably more like 150, it now appears to be a mixed oak and hornbeam wood with little to differentiate the standards from the coppice.

When it was managed woodland, the oak standards would be allowed to grow straight to form a sparse canopy, under which regularly coppiced hornbeam stools would provide a supply of wood destined mostly for London's hearths. The oaks would be felled infrequently, and only when they had reached a size large enough to provide straight timber planks for use in construction. Hornbeam coppice poles, on the other hand, would have been cut more frequently, perhaps every 12 to 15 years, and at most 20 years.

Queen's Wood is the first of the ancient woodlands visited on this walk. It is managed by the London Borough of Haringey, which works with the Friends of Queen's Wood, who run regular work parties and other events here.

Hornbeam former boundary tree

2 – Highgate Wood and Parkland Walk (North)

Cross Muswell Hill Road and enter Highgate Wood by the New Gate. This is a dramatic entrance to the wood, the path sloping up from the pavement of Muswell Hill Road and into the trees, which from this angle appear particularly monumental. Once in the wood, continue along the Capital Ring as it hugs the road close to the woodland edge.

To your left, beyond some thorn hedging, lies an area of coppice. According to the maps at each entrance, this area was last cut in 2002, and is now almost indistinguishable from the rest of the wood. Its coppicing appears to have been somewhat half-hearted, or maybe there had been too long a gap between harvests, but very few multi-stemmed coppice stools are visible. Beyond the coppiced area the path splits: a wooden sign points left to the café and toilets, but you should continue straight on past Keeper's Cottage. An ornate Victorian Hansel-and-Gretel-style mock Tudor building, built by the Corporation of London in 1886 when it took on the management of the wood, it still provides seemingly idyllic accommodation for a lucky employee.

Note the array of mature conifers surrounding the cottage, a throwback to the days when the wood was managed as a park – a practice only ended in 1968. Today's conservationists might consider these exotic trees a strange choice for a native wood, but back in the nineteenth century they would have been considered picturesque, compared to the surrounding working landscape of a managed woodland.

Ignore another turning immediately after the cottage and continue straight on, past another area of coppice on your left, this time, last cut in 1997. Soon you reach Onslow Gate, beyond which an ancient earthwork is just discernible. A shallow ditch marked by a large **Oak** to the left of the path is the start of a feature that runs straight through the wood. It is unclear what this was for, or how old it is; unlike the wood bank in Queen's Wood, it does not appear to mark a former boundary.

Beyond the earthwork continue along the path behind houses on your right, and leave the wood at the Cranley Gate past a pair of **Hazels**. Hazel would once have

Keeper's Cottage

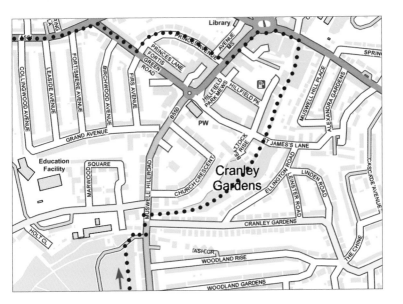

been a part of the coppiced understorey of Highgate Wood. A naturally multi-stemmed shrub, it was an important source of poles used for fencing, wattle and daub construction, and in Kent especially for hop poles. In London, hazel's importance was secondary to hornbeam, which was used for firewood and charcoal.

As you re-emerge onto the broad pavement of Muswell Hill Road, turn left past a large **Ash** tree growing out of the pavement. It is something of a conundrum: could it once have been part of Highgate Wood? Was it planted here, or maybe it grew of its own accord when this edgeland was less well tended? As any London gardener will know, Ash displays particular fecundity in disturbed ground, springing up in flower beds, lawns and railway embankments.

Just before the bus stop, take the sloping path to the left and descend to an

Formerly coppiced Hornbeam

Highgate Wood

Highgate Wood has a rather different character to Queen's Wood, although their species are very similar. For a start, it's flatter, and this makes its monumental oaks seem particularly huge.

The effects of past coppicing are more noticeable here too. The frequent Hornbeams are tall and old, and many have more than one trunk. Like Queen's Wood, it is another ancient woodland, and would have been managed on a similar regime of coppice with standards.

It was handed to the Corporation of London in the late nineteenth century for the enjoyment of all Londoners, and has been managed by it as a woodland nature reserve for the last fifty years or so. Prior to that, it was managed as an urban park, R. S. R. Fitter noting in 1945 in *London's Natural History* that Highgate Wood 'has no undergrowth, except for a few scanty brambles, and its floor is as bare of vegetation as any fir plantation'. It is heartening to witness how nature has returned since then.

There are several large, and elusive, Wild Service Trees in the woods, along with some exceptionally good Pedunculate Oaks and many fine Hornbeams. Midland Hawthorn is frequent, along with Common Hawthorn. The former is an ancient woodland indicator species particularly adapted to life in shady woods. It is distinguishable from its sibling species by having less indented leaves, and berries which hold multiple seeds. Common Hawthorn berries hold just one.

Highgate Woods is also home to one of London's best displays of bluebells, which can be seen towards the Bridge Gate. While these are not as entrancing as the carpets of flowers found in some Home Counties woodlands, just a few decades ago they were practically non-existent. Since then they have been making a slow recovery – 'gradual' being a common characteristic of how ancient woodland indicator species spread. Come back in a century to see them at their best!

Canary Wharf from the Parkland Walk

underpass signposted as Parkland Walk (North). Under the bridge you join a linear local nature reserve which you follow nearly to its end at Alexandra Park. Before then, around 400 metres from the Cranley Gardens entrance, the path continues over a viaduct as it ascends to Muswell Hill.

As it crosses St James's Lane, much of the vegetation has been cleared to enable walkers to take in the magnificent view. Above us is the stout spire of St James's Church, while to the right a fantastic panoramic view opens up south-eastwards over the city. Three distinct high-rise clusters can be seen: Stratford in the east, Canary Wharf in the centre and, in the west, the towers of the City just peeping out over the Highgate ridge from where this walk started.

Among the shrubs kept on a tight pruning regime along this vantage point are **Gorse**, with dazzling yellow flowers which at certain times of year can smell of coconut, **Hawthorn**, **Blackthorn**, **Bramble** and **Holly**. But look carefully among this thicket and you may spot an imposter. Saplings of the evergreen **Holm Oak** have leaves very similar to holly –indeed, both their common and botanical names refer to holly: 'holm' is

an old English name for holly, while 'ilex' is its Latin genus name.

Holm Oak originates in the western Mediterranean and the Atlantic coast of France, and has long been planted here. London's climate, it seems, is much to its liking, and Holm Oak can now be frequently seen popping up in untended corners across town. It is not infrequent along the Parkland Walk, and longer- established examples can be seen displaying leaves that have lost their holly-like spikes, and are mature enough to produce the slender acorns typical of this species.

Continue along the Parkland Walk, passing on the right, midway along, an splendid and unmissable **Oak** tree. It sits high on the former railway embankment, its roots exposed by decades of climbing and swinging by generations of local kids.

Just before the Parkland Walk dives under busy Muswell Hill and into Alexandra Park, take the path out of the woods to the right and onto the street. Walk uphill past 77 Muswell Hill and its attendant **Hornbeam** street tree – a young specimen that nods to the species that defines London's ancient woodlands.

3 – Muswell Hill to Coldfall Wood

Continue up the hill past the Mossy Well pub – named for a spring that once rose here, and of which the River Moselle is a corruption – and you arrive in the heart of prosperous, Edwardian Muswell Hill. Edwardian shopping parades fan out from the roundabout-cum-bus-stand at its centre, from where you turn left into Muswell Hill Broadway before crossing the road and turning down grand Princes Avenue.

Along with nearby Queens Avenue, this street, when it was first built, would have been one of Muswell Hill's most sought-after residential addresses. Large detached and semi-detached houses set well back from the street are shaded by neatly pollarded **London Plane** trees, particularly as the street curves round to join Fortis Green

Road. These trees are contemporary with the houses, and would once have been evenly spaced along the length of the street. Sadly, late-twentieth-century demand for car parking and driveways has diminished the street's Edwardian character, and in places forced the removal, without replacement, of many trees. This seems a great shame, as the trees not only add character to the street, but also connect the architecture to the original Edwardian vision of a leafy suburb.

On the corner of Princes Avenue and Fortis Green Road, look in on the small public garden centred around a young **Deodar Cedar** which might one day be a magnificent sight. It was planted to replace a large tree that was itself a survivor of an extensive

Princes Avenue

garden belonging to one of the large country homes that once made up what is now Muswell Hill. When the suburb was built, this corner and its landmark tree were retained; now the garden has no name, and the story of this tree may soon be forgotten.

Across the road, an Arts and Crafts block of flats is complemented by mature **London Planes**, while Firs Avenue next to it, a less grand Edwardian turning, also has many original Planes. As a narrower street, typical of many in Muswell Hill, with houses closer to the path, it sees its trees pollarded very frequently to be kept even smaller than those on Princes Avenue.

Continue west along Fortis Green Road under a mixed canopy including several purple-leaved **'Spaethii' Sycamore** cultivars, until the junction with Fortis Green and Queens Avenue. Turn slightly left here into Fortis Green, past a civic planter resplendent with exotic **Cabbage Palms** and a **Chusan Palm**. After 100 metres, cross the road and turn right into Twyford Avenue, a street announced by heavily pollarded **Hybrid Poplars** on either side. As tidy Twyford Avenue curves round, Fortismere School's playing fields offer an open vista north to Friern Barnet. Only a century ago, this would have been rural woods and farmland.

Turn right down Ringwood Avenue, a street of solid 1930s houses, and head gently downhill to Creighton Avenue. While Ringwood Avenue's street trees are not particularly remarkable – attractive **'Fastigiata' Hornbeams** give way to deathly purple-leaved **'Crimson King' Norway Maples** (something of a staple in Haringey) – several houses appear to have large oaks

Parkland Walk

The Parkland Walk is a former railway line that ran from Finsbury Park to Alexandra Palace. Now it is a green route split into two parts, North and South, divided by an inaccessible section between Highgate and Cranley Gardens.

Cranley Gardens Station, 1909

The railway ceased operations in 1972, and the Parkland Walk was opened to the public in 1984. Since then it has become a much-used and prized local amenity, and home to a wide range of plants and animals, including a large bat population.

It is interesting to compare the Parkland Walk with the ancient woodlands on this route, to see the differences between a newly established woodland and one that's been around for centuries. Here Sycamore is the dominant tree species, along with Ash, Oak, and Hawthorn, while Horse Chestnut, False Acacia, Holm Oak, Hybrid Poplar, Wild Cherry and Silver Birch put in guest appearances. Ancient woodland indicator species are not present, and even hornbeam is all but absent.

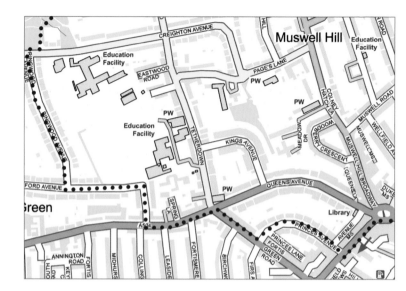

nestling in their back gardens. These are no doubt survivors from the original extent of the next tract of ancient woodland on this route, Coldfall Wood.

The wood's southern edge is now defined by Creighton Avenue, but until the early twentieth century it extended as far south as Fortis Green: the suburban 1930s streets of Ringwood Avenue, Beech Drive and Church Vale cover what was, until less than 100 years ago, an ancient woodland twice its current size. It is unthinkable now that such a fate would be allowed to befall the surviving northern section of Coldfall Wood.

Cross Creighton Avenue and turn right for 50 metres to the gated entrance of the diminished Coldfall Wood. The landscape here is quite unlike the previous woodlands on this route. Large oak trees preside over an extensive and impenetrable tangle of brambles and thorn. Oak standards have

been left to continue their upward growth, while the understorey has been coppiced. The effect is an open, boisterous woodland alive with insects and plants, while jays swoop between canopies and woodpeckers hammer in the distance.

This vision of a working past doesn't last long, however. Soon you are in a deep,

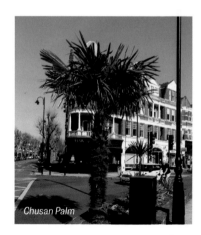

Chusan Palm

dark woodland with little ground flora. Eerie, twisted **Hornbeams** surround larger oaks much as in Queen's and Highgate Woods, but the hornbeams are smaller here, and most have two or three distinct trunks. Coppicing ended later here than in those other woods, and the former stools are still clearly discernible – perhaps they were last cut a mere 90 years ago.

As you enter this deep woodland, veer slightly right to follow the tarmacked path as it hugs the eastern edge. After about 300 metres, the gloom of the wood is lightened by a dazzling green patch to the left, an area of recent coppicing where regeneration from stumps can clearly be seen. Herbaceous plants thrive in a space newly exposed to sunlight, and tree species like **Silver Birch**, **Sallow** and **Rowan** are able to – temporarily – assert themselves. A little

Woodbank, Coldfall Wood

Muswell Hill

Muswell Hill sits atop the gravel high ground of north London with fine views south over the capital. The architecturally coherent Edwardian suburb was developed in the first decade of the twentieth century with a range of housing styles reflecting differing levels of middle-class affluence.

Queen's Avenue

Trees were an integral part of the suburb's development, and hundreds of street trees planted over a hundred years ago can still be seen. These centurions are all London Planes, the tree city planners then were enamoured with.

Following the opening of the tree-lined Victoria Embankment in the early 1870s, London had woken up to the charms of city trees for providing both shade and ornament. From the late nineteenth century through to the start of the First World War, civic leaders were determined to emulate what had previously been a continental European practice. Consequently, any new city streets were incomplete without a complement of trees, and none deemed more suitable than the London Plane.

Coldfall Wood from Ringwood Avenue

further on, the path appears to be exiting the wood. Take the left fork off the tarmac here, into what an interpretation board describes as wet woodland. A boardwalk takes you through an area of **Willows** and muddy pools to emerge next to a clearly apparent wood bank.

The path follows the wood bank, now on your left, which snakes around the northern perimeter of the wood and is dotted along its length with remarkable twisted **Hornbeams**. Eventually the path crosses a small wooden bridge so the wood bank is now on your right, on the very edge of the wood fulfilling one of its original purposes of demarcating the boundary. The primary purpose of wood banks, however, was to keep animals out. For hundreds of years, Coldfall Wood was surrounded by arable farmland, and keeping the tongues of

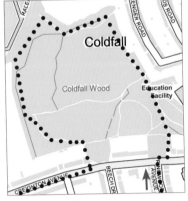

voracious cattle away from tasty regenerating coppice shoots was, no doubt, a constant battle. The path curves round past the recently encouraged reedbed, an area of boggy ground on the route of the stream that runs through the wood, and ascends to exit on Creighton Avenue.

Ancient Woodland

Wild Service Tree

Ancient woodlands are those documented to have been in existence since at least 1600. Before this, few new woods were planted, so it's likely any appearing in the records at this time could go back much further, possibly as far as the first wildwood that colonised these islands after the last ice age.

Another sure way to tell if a wood is very old is the presence of 'ancient woodland indicator species' – plants, sometimes rare and often shy, that have co-existed in woodlands for millennia. Unlike their more promiscuous cousins like Sycamore, Buddleia and Tree of Heaven, that will colonise railway embankments and other disturbed ground at the drop of a hat, they need very specific conditions, and the close relationships they build up with the rest of the plant community create the character of ancient woodlands.

Indicator species might include Wild Service Trees, Midland or Woodland Hawthorn, bluebells and wood anemone. Not all of these need to be present, and many other species that fall into this category, but these four are most likely to be seen in north London's ancient woods.

London's pockets of ancient woodlands will have been managed in the past to provide wood for fuel, timber for construction, grazing for livestock or a habitat for deer. In part, this is how they have survived, seemingly against the odds, for so many centuries.

Coppicing is the most frequently encountered woodland management regime. It is a sustainable practice whereby trees are cut back to their bases, allowing the regrowth of new shoots harvested every 12-20 years. Coppice stools can be very old indeed, as regular management prolongs their lifespan. If trees are not coppiced for many years they will develop into large trees often with more than one primary trunk, a habit much seen in the woods on this walk.

4 – Creighton Avenue to Highgate Tube station

Cross over Creighton Avenue and continue west past Church Vale until, 200 metres further on, a turquoise sign welcomes you to the London Borough of Barnet, next to which a gap between the houses leads on to Durham Road, lined with older houses than those you have just passed. The back gardens mark the nineteenth-century south-western edge of Coldfall Wood.

There is little to detain you on this street save a handful of small street trees, mostly **Juneberries**, or Amelanchiers, a neat, subsidence-proof tree much planted in this part of Barnet. At the end of Durham Road, take a dog-leg over the very old-established thoroughfare of Fortis Green and turn into Summerlee Avenue, an early twentieth-century street partly planted with elegant **Silver Birches**. It is conceivable that this street was planted with birches when it was first constructed, but, the species being relatively short-lived, the trees now lining it are likely to be second- or third-generation.

Where Summerlee Avenue meets Southern Road, turn right and then, past a group of **Purple Cherry Plums** (at their finest in March when they are covered in delicate pink or white blossom), turn into **Juneberry**-lined Ingram Road (where these flowering trees will be at their fleeting best in mid-April). At the end of Ingram Road, turn right onto partially unmade Brompton Avenue, which leads to a path opening onto East Finchley High Road.

Art-Deco East Finchley station is across the road, complete with a stylised stone archer aiming his arrowless bow straight

down the southbound track of the Northern Line. An urban myth suggests that the arrow is buried at the line's southern terminus in Morden.

Close to where you have emerged lies the well-concealed entrance to Cherry Tree Wood, where you rejoin the Capital Ring. An interpretation board explains that it is now a park, but was formerly an ancient woodland. Initially the ancient woodland legacy is clear – some old oaks and twisted hornbeams are similar to those seen in the other woods on this walk – but they soon give way to open grass. The park is small and wedge-shaped, and the path quickly forks. Taking the left fork, pass several **Wild Cherry** trees with their distinctive shiny bark marked with horizontal lenticels. Wild cherry (or gean) is, along with **Blackthorn** and **Bird Cherry**, one of our native *Prunus* species. Wild cherries

can become very large trees, and their attractive white blossom in April can be an arresting sight in woodland glades. Both other species are here too: blackthorn – the source of sloes – forms dense thickets joyously coated in March in tiny white flowers, while bird cherry is the last to flower, putting out blooming spikes from late April.

The park opens up into a large grassy area, with pockets of woodland relegated to its edges. Perhaps these could be regarded as refugia from where in the future the park's woodland character could be reclaimed. As our path reaches the far side of Cherry Tree Wood, more park-like features appear: a café and tennis courts. Just beyond the café stands a fine example of a tree that has been present but elusive in all the other ancient woodlands.

It is a **Wild Service Tree**, an ancient woodland indicator species. Related to the rowan and the whitebeam, it has distinctive spiky leaves rather like a hawthorn. Its exposed location, where it must have been planted, enables these to be examined, along with creamy flowers in early May and

Wild Cherry

Hornbeam

Carpinus betulus

Hornbeam may not be as familiar as the ubiquitous London Plane, but if there is one tree species most associated with London, it is this one. Found in all of London's ancient woodlands, it is historically a constituent of semi-natural woods growing in an arc of southern England from Kent to Hertfordshire, with London right in the middle of its territory.

Its name is derived from 'horn', synonymous with 'hard', and 'beam', an old English word for wood or tree. It's a functional name given to a tree prized for its hard timber, whose presence would be particularly useful in a working woodland close to a centre of population. Hornbeam wood was regularly harvested as relatively small-diameter poles, processed into short lengths suitable for firewood or for manufacturing small items like tool handles or charcoal.

While Hornbeam grows well in London, it's a shy tree when it comes to reproduction. It will happily disperse seedlings in ancient woodlands, but rarely beyond the confines of these rarefied environments: it won't be found on a railway embankment, and very rarely in the relatively natural habitat being created on the Parkland Walk.

Hornbeams should be regarded as an important part of London's natural heritage: not only an essential characteristic of ancient woodland, they have also, over the millennia since they arrived in Britain, been busy building up relationships with a wealth of other wildlife, to the extent that they now support a greater diversity of fungi, insects, plants, birds and small mammals than any other tree species in the city including the mighty oak.

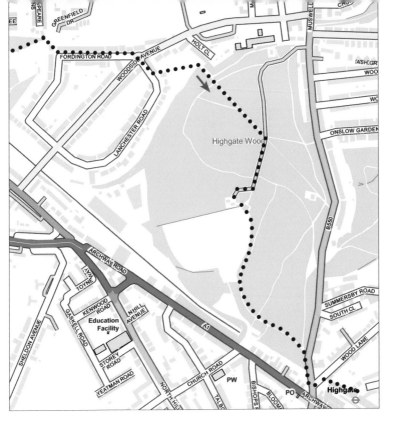

brown berries which ripen in October. This relatively young tree has not yet developed chequered bark, a feature of some older trees found by the very eagle-eyed in the depths of Queen's, Highgate and Coldfall Woods.

Leave the park via a gate onto Fordington Road, along which you continue straight ahead until the mini-roundabout and the junction with Woodside Avenue and Lanchester Road. A green triangle at the corner of Fordington Road and Woodside Avenue is worth stopping for. A pair of domed **Stone Pines** in an adjoining front garden rub shoulders with a **Dawn Redwood**, an increasingly popular deciduous conifer,

and a particularly broad **Norway Maple**.

At the junction, head up posh Lanchester Road where, after about 50 metres, the Capital Ring is signposted between two houses leading back into Highgate Wood. Before taking this path, it is worth admiring the garden dominated by a large **Copper Beech**. But look a little closer for the multi-trunked **Hornbeam**: reminiscent of many we have seen on this walk and, like the back garden oaks of Ringwood Avenue, a reminder of the once far greater reach of these north London woodlands.

It can only be hoped that current redevelopment spares the old **Black Mulberry** hanging over a back garden fence

Victorian Drinking Fountain

onto the Capital Ring. . . The path flattens
out onto a bridge which crosses the course
of the now- disused railway looping round
Highgate Wood which at Cranley Gardens
becomes the Parkland Walk. Continue into
the wood via the Bridge Gate.

Once back in the woods, the path
continues straight ahead, and in April a
large glade of bluebells can be admired
to its left. After 200 metres you reach the
Victorian Drinking Fountain, a polished
granite obelisk. A plaque recalls it was 'The
Gift of a few Friends. Erected 1888', while
a second plaque bears an inscription from
Samuel Taylor Coleridge, a former Highgate
resident:

*Drink, Pilgrim, here! Here rest! And if thy
heart*
Be innocent, here too shalt thou refresh
Thy spirit, listening to some gentle sound
Or passing gale or hum of murmering bees!

From here you fork off to the right and,
after 100 metres, ignore the Capital Ring
sign to the left. Instead continue straight
on to the excellent café, a recommended
refreshment stop overlooking the playing
fields and next to the information hut.
Continue through the trees behind the information hut – essential for anyone interested
in learning more about the wood. Following

the edge of the playing fields, the path curves round past the children's playing area on the right, eventually leading to the exit at Gypsy Gate.

About 70 metres before the gate, a **Wild Service Tree**-bagger will want to stop and look carefully for a good specimen nearby. It has the characteristic chequered bark (from which some say another popular name derives: the chequer tree), and three distinct trunks. In many ways it is no larger than the Cherry Tree Wood specimen, but it is surely much older if the multiple trunks are a legacy of it having once been coppiced. Leave the wood on Muswell Hill Road and turn right. Cross at the traffic lights and arrive at the Woodman pub, which by now

Midland Hawthorn

may be an appealing sight. To complete the walk, though, turn onto Wood Lane, where a signposted path descends to the Priory Gardens entrance of Highgate Tube station.

Bluebells in Highgate Wood

Tree of Heaven and column capital, Vestry Road, Walthamstow

Surprising Trees Between River and Forest

A Walthamstow Circular

For those who have never been, Walthamstow comes
as something of a surprise. Historically part of Essex, it is
hemmed in by the River Lea and its marshes to the west,
and by Epping Forest on its eastern flank. Over the years,
it has developed a unique character, at once fizzing with
energy and preserving vestiges of its past. In less than 200
years it has been transformed from an agrarian parish into
a densely populated London suburb.
On this route, Walthamstow's trees will define a fascinating
corner of London and uncover its layers of history.

Length: 5 miles (10,500 steps)
Start and Finish: Walthamstow Central Tube station
Shortening: Head back to Walthamstow Central from the William Morris Gallery
Accessibility: Pavements and level surfaces, crossing some busy roads and a park
Relative Difficulty: 3/5

1 – Planetree Path to the Warner Estate

This walk starts on Planetree Path, a pedestrian route off Selborne Road between Walthamstow Central's bus station, also an exit for Tube and Overground lines, and a branch of Tesco.

Unsurprisingly, Planetree Path is lined with **London Planes**. They have probably been here for a century or more and, as swellings in the branches show, have in the past been pollarded 4 or 5 metres above ground. Pollarding urban trees is a time-honoured practice, still regularly carried out on larger urban trees.

Arboreal fashions change, though, along with the severity of pollarding regimes. The Planetree Path trees would once have been kept as relatively small trees, but at some point it was decided to let them grow, the former pollard 'knuckles' marking where two or three thick branches now divide, and where once a thicket of stems would have sprouted. These historical nodes are visible on older trees all over London.

The path clings to the eastern edge of the bus station before turning left and ending on Rosebank Villas, a short and extravagantly paved passage onto Walthamstow High Street. The recently redeveloped eastern end of the High Street now boasts dazzlingly white-trunked **Himalayan Birches**, a species that, judging by its popularity in new developments, is the tree of choice for twenty-first-century planners.

Turn left on the High Street heading west past the library and Town Square, shaded by maturing **London Planes**. Every day except Sunday and Monday, this marks the start of Walthamstow's bustling outdoor

Planetree Path

market, Europe's longest, stretching west for a kilometre. The busy market coupled with the narrow street are the reason why you won't see street trees planted beyond this point.

Continue along the High Street for about 200 metres before turning right into Truro Road and, after 50 metres, right again into Eldon Road. On the left, look out for a mature purple-leaved **'Spaethii' Sycamore**. A type of maple, sycamores are very frequent in London, seeding themselves wherever they can, much to the annoyance of some. This purposefully planted tree is an example of the 'Spaethii' cultivar, a peculiarly

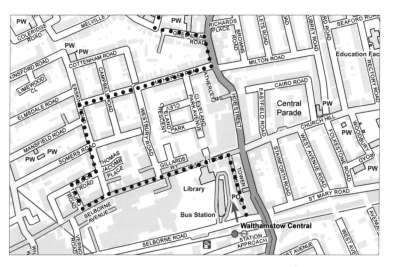

popular choice in some parts, despite the rather dark and overbearing hue of its leaves. Further along and on the other side of the road, another row of Maples demands scrutiny. These are an altogether more unusual variety, **'Palmitifidum'**, a rare cultivar of **Norway Maple** with very deeply cut leaves that might confound even the most experienced maple identifier.

Just past these trees, turn left onto Er-

'Palmitifidum' Norway Maple

skine Road, which you should follow for 100 metres before turning right into Hatherley Road. The residential streets of this part of Walthamstow are lined with a haphazard mix of trees, clearly planted in piecemeal fashion. Despite being constructed during the height of the street-tree-planting era around the turn of the nineteenth and twentieth centuries, streets like these, built for working families, would have been unlikely to benefit from the new craze. As Harold Dyos, a historian writing about Camberwell in the nineteenth century put it,

Planes and horse chestnuts for the wide avenues and lofty mansions of the well-to-do; limes, laburnums and acacias for the middle incomes; unadorned macadam for the wage-earners.

Hatherley Road has a rather pedestrian selection of birches, cherries, a **Chanticleer Pear** or two and some **Purple Cherry**

Waltham Forest

Walthamstow Town Hall

Walthamstow lies at the heart of the London Borough of Waltham Forest, an urban area of north-east London also including Chingford, Leyton and Leytonstone. So where is the Forest?

The name Waltham Forest remembers an ancient forest jurisdiction that once covered a much larger area than the current London borough. In fact, its boundaries included today's Epping and Hainault Forests and extended further east and north as far as Harlow in Essex.

While it was called a forest, it was not entirely covered with trees; instead it would have been a patchwork of woods, wood pasture and grassland.

The notion of forests was introduced to England by the conquering Normans. Their primary purpose was to provide hunting for the monarch. Royal hunting forests had a raft of secondary uses too, including grazing for livestock and a sustainable source of wood. Forests – essentially enclosed landscapes where game animals could roam freely – had their own laws and a significant bureaucracy to uphold them.

The open landscapes of Wanstead Flats or Chingford Plain are fairly close to what would have covered the treeless parts of Waltham Forest, and what is now Walthamstow, in the Middle Ages. These areas of wood pasture are part of the rich tapestry of landscapes that make up today's Epping Forest, a remnant of Waltham Forest. They are ancient landscapes that come right into the borough and can accurately be called a forest.

So perhaps the modern borough's name is not so inexplicable.

Plums, a staple of municipal planting in some parts. At its end, turn left briefly on to Hoe Street, admiring the conical form of several **Turkish Hazels** on the opposite pavement, and then turn left into Greenleaf Road. Just after Boleyn Close, the roadway is blocked by bollards. This is part of the 'Mini-Holland' development, a scheme rolled out across Waltham Forest to encourage cycling and walking over car use. Elsewhere in the borough, 22 kilometres of cycle lanes have been built, and dozens of car-discouraging road build-outs, ship-loads of bollards

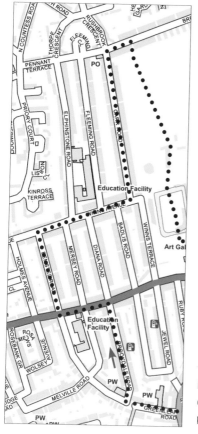

Green Ash

and hundreds of new trees put in place.

Just beyond the bollards, turn left onto Brookdale Road. It curves round to reveal a long, gently sloping street with views north over the Lea Valley flood plain. Here, you will notice, is a consistently planted avenue, the first on this route. The trees here are **Green Ash**, an unusual North American species closely related to our native ash. It differs in having golden autumnal foliage. Although they are infrequent in the UK, it appears someone in Waltham Forest had a penchant for them, and a surprising number have been planted around the borough. Once you complete more of these walks in different parts of London, you'll start to notice how street tree choices often vary between boroughs, reflecting both different approaches by local authorities and the often whimsical predilections of the individuals who have selected and planted them over the years. Brookdale Road ends at the crossroads bisected by Forest Road, the main road through Walthamstow. Turn left, take the zebra crossing, and then continue along Forest Road briefly before turning right into Bemsted Road, part of the Warner Estate.

Immediately the character of the streets has changed. Consistent redbrick terraced houses are complemented by a consistent avenue of **'Fastigiata' Hornbeams**. Behind the front gardens – all too many of which have swapped roses and privet hedges for wheelie bins – look out for houses boasting restored paintwork along with original doors and window frames.

At the end of Bemsted Road, turn right into Winns Avenue, a long road lined entirely with birches. Three different species are here, **Himalayan Birch** and **Erman's Birch** the most common, while one or two **Silver Birches** can be seen too. Each has white bark – Himalayan being the cleanest – and similar leaves, so the best way to tell them apart is by their shapes and overall characteristics. Himalayan have rounded crowns, Silver are tall and willowy with pendulous branches, and Erman's have an upright character and are the first birch to lose their leaves in the autumn.

As Winns Avenue approaches its end, turn left into Carr Road. Still on the Warner Estate, this street bucks the arboreal conformity by hosting a mixed selection of trees including **American Sweetgum**, **Green** and **Raywood Ash**, **Purple Cherry Plum**, **Norway** and **Cappadocian Maple**. It is at its best in the autumn when a fine show of leaf colours can be enjoyed. Turn right off Carr Road into Brettenham Road, where a **Turkish Hazel** and a **'Frisia' False Acacia** are followed by a treeless stretch of pavement. As the terrace of Victorian Warner Estate houses ends on your right, take the passage into Lloyd Park, keeping some mid-twentieth-century houses on your left.

Erman's Birch

The Warner Estate

Bemsted Road

The Warner Estate covers a large area of Walthamstow and is characterised by attractive, high-quality yet affordable housing. It was developed from the late nineteenth century by Courtenay Warner, an aristocrat, army officer and Liberal politician. This walk takes in a swathe of the estate north of Forest Road east to Lloyd Park.

Warner offered housing to people moving to the newly developing suburb of Waltham-stow at rents just above the market rate in order to attract a 'better class' of tenants. Most of the housing was split into maison-ettes with double-front doors under a single archway with shared gardens.

They were built to a high standard and special attention was paid to architectural detailing. Tenancy agreements included clauses stipulating residents were to regularly clean their curtains and maintain neat gardens. Exterior doors and window frames were painted bright green with

highlights picked out in cream. From 1892 trees were planted along the streets and, while few of the originals survive, trees have been replanted here ever since, although the species found now are unlikely to be the same.

Most Warner tenants were smitten with their new homes, and many settled for good. Some people living here today are able to trace their family histories back decades. Over the years, some of the homes have been sold off, but many have passed on to a housing association which continues to rent them out.

2 – Lloyd Park to Hoe Street

Lloyd Park is the green focus of Walthamstow. There are two distinct parts: a southern more formal area and northern playing fields, which is where you arrive from Brettenham Road. This area, formerly known as Aveling Fields, was previously farmland, the rows of mature **Common Limes** marking old field boundaries.

Follow the path due south past the skate park and the café, making a detour to admire the mature **Golden Rain Tree** between the kids' adventure playground and the café's eastern entrance. Eventually, you pass through the screen of Lime trees and enter the southern part of Lloyd Park. While this too is demarcated into different areas, it has been the garden of the Georgian Water House for at least 250 years. Cross the tarmacked carriageway (a feature of many Victorian parks), and over the footbridge spanning the water-filled moat onto the rectangular island.

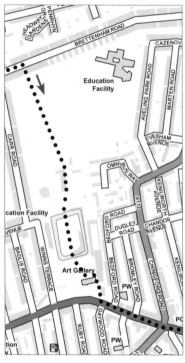

Lloyd Park Plane

The moat is a medieval feature which would once have surrounded a long-gone manor house. Now, it is surrounded by a mix of trees, including **Yew**, **Lime**, **Sycamore** and some **Holm Oaks**, mostly planted when the park opened in 1900. It's hard to imagine the genteel, and rather shallow, moat as a defensive feature, although the island it now surrounds feels something of a haven. A small copse of **English Walnuts** is noteworthy before you cross the moat again to arrive in formal gardens to the rear of Water House, now the William Morris Gallery.

To your right a magnificent **London**

Plane towers over the herbaceous borders of a raised terrace, where a splendidly isolated **Snow Gum** dominates, a species of Australian eucalypt with particularly attractive bark. Beyond the characterful brick wall in front of you, a striking columnar poplar is visible – this is a **Plantière Poplar**, a type commonly mislabelled as **Lombardy Poplar**. While Lombardy Poplars are popular in more southerly latitudes, they have largely been supplanted by Plantières in England, which are more robust and better adapted to the British climate than the very similar Italian tree.

Head straight ahead through the formal gardens towards the Gallery and turn left along its northern perimeter. Just beyond the Gallery's café, The Larder (a recommended refreshment stop), turn right to leave the gardens past a **Judas Tree**. Once you are through the gate, notice the **Southern Catalpa** or Indian Bean Tree hanging over the old brick wall to your left,

and a **Yew** to your right. Continue across the gravel driveway to the exit onto Forest Road. You pass a fine **Pedunculate Oak** tree next to the entrance, and beyond it to your right you may be struck by an ornamental curiosity, a **Young's Weeping Birch**, a cultivar of silver birch.

Turn left on Forest Road and, after a few metres, take the zebra crossing to its southern side, where a red plaque is attached to the low brick wall in front of a modern low-rise building. The plaque introduces the **Strawberry Tree**, of which four young examples can be seen in the gardens between the building and the pavement. The leaves and fruit of the tree feature in one of William Morris's most popular designs known as Arbutus, the Latin name for the strawberry tree genus.

If you want to split this walk in two halves, this is a good point to do so: you can head straight down Hoe Street for 800 metres back to Walthamstow Central.

William Morris Gallery and Young's Weeping Birch

Water House and William Morris

Arbutus pattern wallpaper

Water House is a handsome Georgian mansion constructed in 1760, now more commonly known as the William Morris Gallery. Textile designer, early socialist and Walthamstow's most famous son, William Morris lived at Water House as a teenager between 1848 and 1856.

Known as Water House because of its moated island, the house and gardens were handed to the local council in 1898 by its last private owner, Frank Lloyd, becoming Lloyd Park in 1900, with Water House opening as the William Morris Gallery in 1950. Since then it has become a major visitor attraction and destination for anyone interested in the life and work of the romantic and complex figure of William Morris.

The wealthy Morris family downsized to Water House in the country village of Walthamstow from the considerably larger Woodford House set in 50 acres adjacent to Epping Forest.

Much of Morris's work, particularly his textile designs, exhibits a sensitivity to nature, an awareness surely fostered by his childhood environment of garden, forest, field and water. Within these nineteenth-century working landscapes, Morris would have been aware of the labour practices that had existed for generations: an awareness that was to inform his later socialism and the esteem he held for traditional crafts.

3 – Forest Road to Wood Street

Continue east along Forest Road passing a **Tulip Tree** in the pavement just before Hawthorne Road, which you cross before arriving at the busy junction with Hoe Street. Continue over the junction and, after 50 metres, turn right into Falmer Road, which rises steeply. It's lined with a good crop of street trees, among which you might notice in autumn the bright red foliage of several **American Sweetgums**.

At the brow of the hill, turn left on Seaford Road. A short detour into Rectory Road on your right is worthwhile to see a **Red Maple** in the pavement and an **Aspen** hanging over from the school playground. Back on Seaford Road, admire the view north over Waltham Forest's grand 1930s town hall to the edge of London and open countryside beyond. Just beyond Hurst Road, Seaford Road becomes The Drive, which confusingly also turns off to the right, but you continue straight ahead.

The Drive is a magnificent street lined with mature **London Planes** creating a vaulted green cathedral. This was once among the most sought-after addresses in Walthamstow, and was lined with several large houses which would have enjoyed the fine views to the north. They are long gone, replaced by a 1950s estate. The estate blocks, some with botanical names like Poplar, Maple and Hibiscus, are surrounded by mature gardens with many trees. Among them are some fine conifers, which lend a distinctly central European ambience.

At the end of The Drive you will notice a Georgian brick building on the opposite side of Shernhall Street. This is Walthamstow House, now part of the Holy Family Catholic School, but formerly one of the grand private residences that were once a feature of rural Walthamstow before its nineteenth-century expansion. Turn right on Shernhall Street, crossing it and turning left

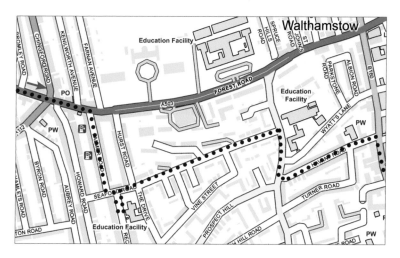

Plane canopy of The Drive

you turn left into Wood Street. Sheltering under its spreading canopy, as if to emphasise its scale, is a white weatherboard building, once a village butcher's, and now a healthfood shop. The shop is over 200 years old, and the tree not much younger. It has been a much-loved landmark for many years, and in 1987 was voted a Great Tree of London, joining an illustrious list.

Navigate the zebra crossing to get the best view of it, and turn right to head south on Wood Street, a thriving local shopping street with a mix of traditional shops, new eateries, well-established pubs and the Wood Street Indoor Market, an institution in these parts. On the tree front, however, there is not much to detain you: some well-spaced **Field Maples** have been planted on the pavement, and mature trees can be glimpsed down side streets.

on Havant Street, a street lined with **Turkish Hazels** interspersed with some **Chanticleer Pears**.

As you approach the end of Havant Street, you will notice a group of large trees on your left just before the junction with Wood Street. First among these is a mature **Sycamore**, but the largest is a magnificent **Horse Chestnut**.

It becomes all the more impressive as

Wood Street Horse Chestnut

Horse Chestnut

Aesculus hippocastanum

We're fond of Horse Chestnut trees. They are easily recognisable and familiar features of our landscapes and cityscapes. In London they tend to be found in parks and gardens, and sometimes on the street. Many older trees have survived from earlier planting schemes, especially in the outer boroughs where large, country villas have disappeared but the denizens of their former gardens have remained.

Maybe our fondness for Horse Chestnuts derives in part from memories of childhoods spent collecting and playing conkers. Showy springtime flower candles gladden the hearts too, while their striking palmate, or hand-shaped, five-fingered leaves have become iconic. Indeed, Waltham Forest's neighbouring borough, Redbridge, uses a Horse Chestnut leaf in its logo.

Sadly, Horse Chestnuts are under threat on several fronts, most severely from a bacterial canker that causing the bark on some trees to 'bleed' and become disfigured, ultimately leading to the tree's death.

But the most conspicuous problem is leaf miners: tiny caterpillars eating the leaves from the inside, causing them to become brown and disfigured by mid-summer. While unsightly, it doesn't kill the trees, and each spring they will, miraculously, burst back into life.

As a result of the problems Horse Chestnuts face, they are rarely, if ever, planted these days, so we should enjoy them while we can. If any tree could be described as old-fashioned, it is Horse Chestnut, inducing nostalgia for childhood and lost idylls of parks and gardens.

4 – Valentin Road to Walthamstow Central via the Village

Just before Wood Street Overground station, turn right onto Valentin Road, noting on its right-hand side the gardens around the blocks of flats, which play host to some interesting trees. In the first bay, there's a **Downy Birch**. Similar to Silver Birch, it's another native species, but has a more upright form without the pendulous young branches of their cousin.

Further along, in a garden next to the bus stop, a very good example of a **'Petiolaris' Silver Lime** cultivar can be seen. Look carefully for the graft union, clearly visible on the tree's trunk about a metre from the ground. These subtly weeping trees were much admired by the Victorians, and good examples can be seen in parks across London. This one is not as large as some in Hyde Park or Brompton Cemetery (see page 158), but it is nevertheless a fine example of an unusual tree. At the end of Valentin Road, turn left briefly on Sternhall Road before continuing straight over on Church Lane.

'Petiolaris' Silver Lime

On Church Lane, just before a **Honey Locust**, turn right onto Vinegar Alley. Follow it as it cuts through the churchyard of St Mary's Church, noting on either side some fine **Sycamores**, **Common Limes** and **Horse**

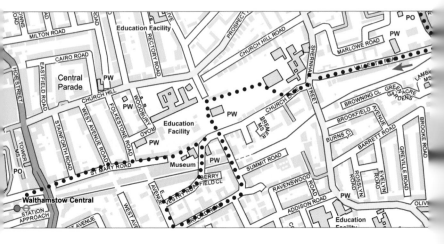

Ancient House from the church

Chestnuts. Just before you draw level with the church, look out for a large **Goat Willow** in the churchyard on your right. The path disgorges you between the church and the much restored sixteenth-century Monoux Almshouses: turn right here through the churchyard, passing many pollarded **Horse Chestnuts** and some striking early-nineteenth-century graves.

You emerge from the churchyard on Church Lane opposite the timber-framed Ancient House, a remarkable fifteenth-century survivor. From here, turn down Orford Road, passing the Nag's Head, opposite which is a terrace of houses facing a thicket of trees, the overgrown railway embankment of the Chingford-to-Liverpool Street Overground line.

Among them is a **Tree of Heaven**, an opportunist hailing from China that is on the march along railway embankments and other edgelands across the city. It is an attractive tree with huge pinnate leaves resembling, with a bit of imagination, palm

fronds, which gives rise to a popular name of Ghetto Palm in some east coast US cities. Trees of Heaven can grow at astonishing rates – a metre or more a year – and reproduce vigorously through seed and sucker. Not far away from this tree, others will be lurking . . .

Continue to follow Orford Road over the railway, past handsome early Victorian houses. There are plenty of trees: planes, pines and hornbeams are frequent, with one or two large, evergreen **Holm Oaks**, another Victorian favourite, and another species that will colonise any available land it can.

Follow Orford Road as it curves to the west. A young **'Excelsum Superbum' Chinese Tree Privet** marks the start of Walthamstow Village's main shopping parade, and just beyond appears the unmissable former town hall, a fabulously overblown Victorian chateau affair. A street made up almost exclusively of boutiques, gastro pubs and chi-chi eateries, Orford Road is famously home to the poshest Spar in town. Before you get to it, pause by the pair of **Austrian Pines** in front of the former National School, and admire the double-trunked **False Acacia** in Walthamstow Village Square across the road.

Turn right at the Queen's Arms onto East Avenue and, after 50 metres, right again onto Vestry Road. As the road curves between the playground and the Sakina Trust mosque housed in the former Post Office sorting office, look out for the trees on the northern side of the road. A row of Plane trees includes a couple of **Oriental Planes**, and further along another row is worth stopping for. These are **Japanese Zelkovas**, an elegant species related to the Elms, but not susceptible to Dutch Elm Disease.

Vestry Road curves round to cross the railway again, and brings us to the excellent Vestry House Museum. The museum runs a programme of changing exhibitions as well as hosting local history artefacts, including a wonderful 1822 map of the parish showing just how rural Walthamstow was a mere

200 years ago. Outside the museum, next to an interesting and incongruous carved stone Ionic capital that once adorned a column of the City of London General Post Office, a large **Tree of Heaven** stands sentinel. Perhaps this is the source of the tree opposite the Nag's Head and the expanding local cluster . . .

As Vestry Road curves round past the museum, take the path to the left of the stone capital, and then hard left onto Church Path, lined with cute English country cottages complete with front gardens stuffed with roses and fruit trees. Church Path emerges on St Mary Road, where a **Himalayan Birch** welcomes us back into modern Walthamstow. Continue straight ahead, noting a trio of **London Planes** on the corner of West Avenue which appear to mark some former property boundary, but now describe a parklet and some old garages.

As you continue down St Mary Road, a few well-distanced white-flowering **'Snow Goose' Cherries** line the southern side; they are very similar to, and possibly interchangeable with, the Japanese **'Umineko'** variety, a name that translates as 'Seagull'. Maybe 'Snow Goose' is a romanticised anglification of a name that doesn't quite have the same resonance in translation.

Eventually St Mary Road ends at the confusing junction of Hoe Street and Selborne Road, which you will need to navigate by making several crossings to return to Walthamstow Central Station. There are two entrances to the station, one on the southern side of Selborne Road, and one in the bus station on the northern side just beyond Planetree Path.

Walthamstow Village

Great Trees of London

The Dorchester Plane, a Great Tree of London

There are many great trees in London, as this book demonstrates. But in 1987, following the Great Storm in October of that year which wrought arboreal carnage across much of south-east of England, a list of official Great Trees of London was inaugurated.

Nominated by and voted on by the public, 41 trees from all corners of the city were awarded Great Tree status. Plaques, some of which are now lost, were installed near each one, and in 2008 a further 20 trees were added by the charity Trees for Cities.

Over the years, some of the Great Trees have succumbed, such as the landmark southern catalpa in St James's churchyard, Piccadilly. There are a lot of oaks and planes on the list, which today don't appear to represent the great diversity of trees in London. Other criteria for greatness, such as a tree's status as a landmark, like the New Cross Gate Giant Redwood (see page 128), or the stories they can tell, like the Salter tree in Bermondsey's Alfred Salter Playground (see page 99), should perhaps be taken into account.

Extensive lists of Great Trees have appeared online, social media has been abuzz with suggestions, and the author of this book has edited a map of 46 noteworthy trees. So it seems London is ready for a new and expanded list of Great Trees. It's clear that the Wood Street Horse Chestnut will feature, and perhaps the Snow Gum in Lloyd Park should be considered?

Newly planted French Tamarisks, Retreat Place

London's Urban Arboretum

A Hackney Circular

For many years, Hackney was synonymous with inner-city deprivation, a symptom of which was an aging and decreasing population of street trees. That started to change at the turn of the millennium, when an ambitious tree-planting programme began, complementing the area's already rich arboreal legacy. In 20 years Hackney has been transformed, and now over 350 different tree species and cultivars can be found, many of which you'd otherwise need to visit a botanical garden to see. Of course, this amazing arboreal diversity reflects the cultural diversity of Hackney, where waves of migration have turned this thriving corner of the East End into one of the most vibrant parts of London.

London has long been a 'world city' and now – certainly in this borough – its trees reflect this.

Length: 3 miles (6,500 steps)
Start and Finish: Hackney Central Overground station
Accessibility: Pavements and level surfaces, crossing some busy roads and a park
Relative Difficulty: 2/5

I – Hackney Central to Sutton House

If you arrive at Hackney Central by train you may notice, as you descend the exit ramp, the unkempt **Elder** tree that grows, seemingly straight out of the tarmac next to the car park fence.

This wildling is unusual in such an urban borough: a reminder that nature will seize any opportunity to put down roots, even in the most unlikely spots. It is perhaps a hangover from Hackney's less salubrious days when unregarded corners were commonplace. Nowadays, though, a raft of exotic (and native) tree species await, seemingly on every street corner . . .

Take the flight of steps off the ramp and head across the car park, or optionally, take the ramp all the way down to Amhurst Road and turn right to the car park. In a small triangle of green in the centre of it lies a young tree, an **American Sweetgum**, a species much planted in Hackney and beyond.

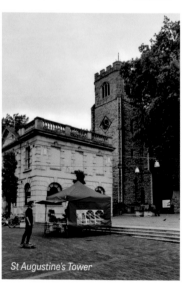

St Augustine's Tower

It has lobed, maple-like leaves, woody seed balls and – the reason for their popularity – fantastic scarlet colouring in the autumn. Beyond the Sweetgum, cross over Amhurst Road to examine a small **Juneberry** fenced in by a black iron tree guard, a design unique to Hackney.

Turn left into Mare Street, heading up the pedestrianised shopping street past the Georgian Old Town Hall and St Augustine's Tower on the right. This is all that remains of Hackney's sixteenth-century parish church, the bulk of which was demolished in 1798 as the new, larger St John-at-Hackney church, just to the north-east, took on that role.

St Augustine's was built when Hackney was a small Middlesex village, and by the late eighteenth century was too small for the swelling parish's rapidly increasing congregation. Since then, of course, Hackney has continued to grow, and the country village of old is barely traceable among this bustling inner-city borough. Interesting newly planted trees abound here: look out for columnar or fastigiate **'Slender Silhouette' American Sweetgums**, **Southern Magnolias**, a **Strawberry Tree** and a cluster of **Persian Ironwoods**.

At the end of Mare Street, cross Dalston Lane, over the recently remodelled central reservation. This is typical of how Hackney Council have been renewing their urban environment, wherever possible including

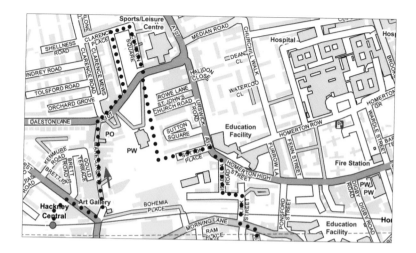

trees, in this case four **Dawn Redwoods**, already a striking landmark. This pedestrian-friendly feature also marks where Dalston Lane becomes Lower Clapton Road, which you follow north-east for 50 metres as it curves round before turning left into Clapton Square.

A classic Regency square with significant infills, notably on the eastern side, Clapton Square's gardens are now open to the general public, a status that differs from many squares in more exclusive parts of London further west. One former resident sets the tone: Theodore Rothstein, journalist and exiled Russian communist, lived here around the turn of the twentieth century, and included Lenin among his visitors.

Lenin would no doubt have enjoyed the square's maturing **London Planes** and **Horse Chestnuts**, and may even have wondered at the identity of a couple of trees found on the eastern side. Until a few years ago, there were three, but now just two rare **True Service Trees** remain. The larger is

just to the left of the gate in the north-east corner, while the other hangs over the pavement towards the south-east.

Closely related to Rowan, or Mountain

True Service Tree

Japanese Pagoda Tree

Ash, trees, True Service trees have very similar pinnate leaves: compound leaves consisting of several leaflets on a single stem. Their flowers are similar too – bunches of small creamy blooms in late April – but that's where the similarities end.

True service trees become much larger, and are far more long-lived than rowans, and instead of red berries they produce larger, rosy, apple- or pear-shaped fruits. They are very much a curiosity, and something of a Hackney peculiar too. In the early nineteenth century, the famous Hackney nursery, Loddiges, was the principal supplier of true service trees, and it could be that this mature specimen was supplied from their nursery just a stone's throw away.

From the southern **True Service Tree**, cross Lower Clapton Road at the zebra crossing and enter St John-at-Hackney's Churchyard Gardens by Churchwell Path. Follow the path down the eastern edge of the churchyard admiring the mature **London Planes**, some of the oldest examples in Hackney, and the moss-covered stone grave vaults. Beyond the church turn left past the Walled Garden with its large Dawn Redwood and a **Southern Catalpa**, emerging onto handsome Sutton Place, a fine Georgian terrace hosting several more **Persian Ironwoods**.

At the end of Sutton Place, turn right onto Homerton High Street and pause outside Hackney's oldest residential building, Tudor Sutton House. It has been owned by the National Trust since the 1930s, but was only restored in the 1990s, having had many recent uses including as a squat during the 1980s.

Across the road from Sutton House, look out for a maturing **Japanese Pagoda Tree**, a species encountered infrequently in London, but one now being increasingly planted for its suitability to a warming climate. If you are following this walk in late July or August, and previous months have been warm, you may be lucky enough to catch it in flower – masses of attractive, and aromatic, white flowers dust its canopy in high summer.

2 – The Chesham Arms to Martello Street

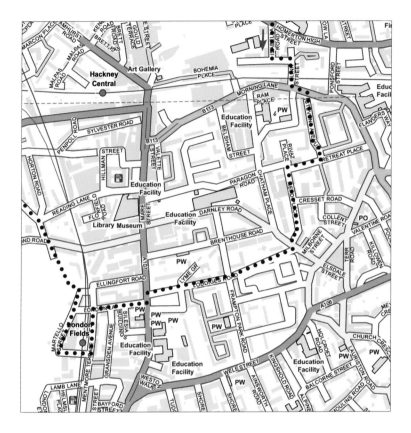

Just to the right of Sutton House, turn right into Isabella Road, a short turning with the cosy-looking, and community managed, Chesham Arms at its end urging you on. Both Isabella and Mehetabel Roads are unusual for Hackney, as they are planted with older street trees that reflect more conservative choices associated with the late twentieth century. Members of the *Sorbus* genus predominate, with both **Whitebeam** and **Bastard Service Tree** present. These will be found elsewhere in

Hackney, but often alongside other, more unusual species.

Turn left on Mehetabel Road and then right onto Link Street, passing another Sorbus, this time a **Rowan** in the garden to the front of Marian Court. Continue under the railway lines and emerge onto busy Morning Lane, turn left to cross at the lights, doubling back on the other side of the road for 50 metres in order to turn into Steven's Avenue. This 'avenue' is in fact a rather narrow, and treeless Victorian terrace, but

The Growth of Hackney

The view from Hackney Downs, 1800s

The place name 'Hackney' variously describes an inner-city London borough, a district within the borough and, for many, just the immediate area around Mare Street and Hackney Central Station. For centuries, Hackney was a largely agricultural parish in Middlesex comprising several villages, of which Hackney 'proper' was the largest.

By the seventeenth century, Hackney was well known for its schools, and is mentioned by the diarist and rogue Samuel Pepys, who records his ulterior motive for a visit to St Augustine's church in 1667: 'That which we went chiefly to see was the young ladies of the schools, whereof there is great store, very pretty.'

During the next century, although still surrounded by fields, Hackney was starting to grow, and it now that Loddiges Nursery was established around what is now the town hall.

In the 1801 census, Hackney's population was just 12,730, but by 1901 it had expanded to a massive 219,272. In the intervening century, its rural character, was lost to Victorian urban sprawl and industrialisation.

The oldest trees in Hackney now are London Plane trees, typified by those around the church, in Clapton Square and the magnificent plantation of London Fields, all of which appeared as the area was developed; none can be much more than 200 years old.

The twentieth century saw wartime destruction, de-industrialisation and waves of migration into Hackney. Stamford Hill's orthodox Jewish community started to arrive in the 1920s, followed by the establishment of vibrant Carribean, Turkish and Vietnamese communities in the decades after the Second World War. By the end of the century, Hackney had the highest concentration of artists anywhere in Europe. It was synonymous with counterculture and inner-city deprivation. Consequently, little money was available for its beautification.

This all started to change in the second half of the 1990s, as the council put in place policies leading to the transformation of the borough. Not least was the appointment of a visionary tree officer, Rupert Bentley-Walls, who was given the political backing, and access to funding, by Mayor Jules Pipe's regime to gradually afforest the borough.

The creation of the Overground, the development of Shoreditch into hipster central, and the 2012 Olympics have all contributed to Hackney's twenty-first century renaissance. Its dizzying nightlife, and its status as a cultural Mecca – both springing from seeds planted in the twentieth century – have made it one of the most sought-after areas of London in which to live, work and play.

For the arboreally-minded, Hackney's transformation is illustrated by Bentley-Walls' tree planting programme and the resulting transformation of streets, estates and parks. Carried out by the council and voluntary groups including the Tree Musketeers, the greening of the borough has been truly remarkable, and is a paradigm for the rest of London. Over 350 species and cultivars reside here, along with a reverence for the area's botanical legacy, and ambitious plans to plant thousands more trees over the next few years. Hackney can rightly claim to be London's urban arboretum.

by way of compensation a pair of variegated **'Silver King' American Sweetgums** guard its entrance. Variegation is a striking ornamental feature seen in many plants including trees, where the leaves are tinged or blotched with white or yellow areas. Variegated sweetgums, though, are very rare – there can be no more than 100 in London.

At the end of Steven's Avenue, turn right onto Retreat Place past a large **London Plane** in a small grassy rectangle surrounded by blocks of low-rise flats. A centurion perhaps, this tree looks older than any of the surrounding buildings and does not appear to have been pollarded in its past, suggesting that it may once have been planted in spacious grounds. Across the road from the plane you will find a newly planted row of four **Wild Service Trees**, a species related to the True Service Tree, but

Steven's Avenue 'Silver King' American Sweetgum

with strikingly different leaves resembling a hawthorn or even a maple. Just beyond, unusual **French Tamarisks** with feathery foliage and pink flowers thoughtfully complement a corrugated metal-clad building (artists' studios). At the end of Retreat Place, turn left onto Mead Place.

Halfway down Mead Place, it is worth taking a short detour down Cresset Road to admire Lennox House, a brick and concrete A-shaped ziggurat resplendent with the date '1937' in cast numerals above a large moulded concrete gateway. Designed by the architect J. E. M. MacGregor for Bethnal Green and East London Housing Association, the flats were conceived as bungalows in the sky, under which a covered market would be housed. That market was very short-lived, and the cavernous space has largely been used as garages.

French Tamarisk, Retreat Place

Back on Mead Place, continue south, admiring the mature trees in the gardens of the Frampton Park Estate to your right. The road curves round to join Elsdale Street, which you should cross to take a closer look at the new trees in the paved area on

Wild Service Tree flowers

Golden Rain Tree

the corner of Loddiges Road. Among them is a young semi-evergreen oak tree. It is a **Spanish Oak**, a hybrid of two Mediterranean species, Turkey and cork oak, sometimes also known as **Lucombe Oak**. However, to be a true Lucombe oak it would need to be a scion of an original tree that arose in the Devon nursery of William Lucombe in 1762. Without a DNA test, or a botanical label, the parentage of this tree is difficult to confirm, but because of its location a thoughtful street-tree-specifier might well have selected a true Lucombe oak.

It is noteworthy for being planted on the corner of Loddiges Road, a street named after a famed Hackney nurseryman. To plant a tree named after one eighteenth-century nurseryman on a street named after another seems more than coincidental. As we have already seen in Clapton Square, echoes of Loddiges' legacy exist elsewhere in Hackney, and this street was built on land that once formed part of their extensive nursery.

Head straight down Loddiges Road for its entire length, continuing beyond the bollards that mark the junction with Frampton Park Road. Improvements to the junction layout here have resulted in widened pavements, allowing for trees to be planted that would have struggled to fit into the original crossroads. Now, Tibetan and **'Amber Beauty' Manchurian Cherries**,

Spanish Oak on Loddiges Road

'Amber Beauty' Manchurian Cherry

cross at the lights just beyond the Square. Double back on the western side in order to turn left into London Lane, admiring a Dawn Redwood planted in Mare Street's central reservation.

On London Lane, just after Silesia Buildings, it is worth stopping to examine a row of **Oriental Planes**. One of the parents of the hybrid London plane, these trees have similar flaking bark, but differ in having more deeply incised leaves and clusters of up to seven seedballs – a London plane typically just has pairs of balls.

Next, turn left into seemingly unremark-able Gransden Avenue, where, in April, a deep-purple-flowering **Lilac** greets you. Further down the street, outside a new terrace of houses, more unusual trees await. The most striking of the bunch is a variegated

'Soviet Tree'

resplendent in their iron tree guards, grace this corner. Beyond, look out for a pair of **Hop Hornbeams** as the road approaches St Thomas's Square.

St Thomas's Square was laid out in 1892, and many of the mature lime and plane trees probably date from that time. Where it joins Mare Street, some younger trees feature, including a mature **Tree of Heaven** – a species in old age at 70, and a **Golden Rain Tree**. Turn left on Mare Street and

Wedding Cake Tree

Wedding Cake Tree, a tree with distinct layers, like a tiered wedding cake. Next to it is another rarity, this one a tree without an English name. It is **x Chitalpa tashkentensis**, a tree developed by Soviet horticulturalists

Hibiscus

during the Cold War, ironically by hybridising two North American trees, the southern catalpa and the desert willow. It produces pink flowers in July and, like most of the mere handful of trees in London, this one has a distinct lean.

Beyond the Soviet tree, a pair of well-spaced **Hibiscus** trees may catch your attention in summer when their big mauve blooms appear. Outside their flowering time they are rather inconspicuous. At the end of Gransden Avenue turn right into Lamb Lane, which you should continue along before taking the next right into Mentmore Terrace just before the railway bridge. Like Gransden Avenue this is another street hiding some unusual trees – a hallmark of contemporary Hackney.

It starts with some fairly standard street trees, but beyond the entrance to London Fields Station, on the eastern side of the street, there's a very striking pair. The first of these is a **Peanut Butter Tree**, or **Harlequin Glorybower**, a small east-Asian tree that has several remarkable proper-

Bee-bee Tree, Mentmore Terrace

ties. It has bunches of wonderfully scented flowers in summer, giving way to odd berries which start white and turn purple, all the while resting on a pink star-shaped cushion. What is less obvious, and from where the peanut butter name is derived, is the leaves: crush one in July and inhale – pure Sunpat. Next to it is a pollinator-friendly **Bee-bee Tree**, another east Asian, and a great rarity. You will only see this tree on the streets of Hackney and in a few botanical collections.

Beyond the Bee-bee Tree, continue straight ahead on Mentmore Terrace until you reach London Lane, where you turn left under the railway and emerge onto Martello Street with London Fields in front of you.

3 – London Fields to Hackney Central

A Hackney institution and favourite summer watering hole, the Pub on the Park greets you as you turn right on Martello Street, and then, after 50 metres, right again onto a footpath, keeping London Fields' children's playground to your right. To your left, the green expanse of London Fields opens up and, if time permits, is well worth exploring. The lido in its north-eastern corner, reopened early in the twenty-first century after decades of dereliction in another of the council's regeneration initiatives, is now a popular attraction all year round.

Just to the south of London Fields, Broadway Market marks the beating heart of hip, gentrifying Hackney. A plethora of trendy bars, bookshops and boutiques rub shoulders with older establishments like Cooke's Pie and Mash and the Dove pub.

Keeping to the path towards the point where it rejoins the street at Eleanor Road, look out for a trio of young **Giant Redwoods**. These are recent plantings compared to the mature **London Plane** trees that abound here, perhaps a mere 20 years old,

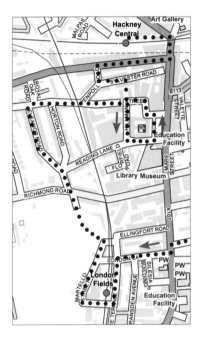

but already their herculean character is discernible.

Shortly, the road joins Richmond Road, where you turn left briefly before crossing to head down the main northern extent of

Giant Redwood foliage

Loddiges of Hackney

Hauling a Mauritius Fan Palm from Loddiges to the Crystal Palace, 1854

By the mid-eighteenth century a German émigré, Johann (John) Busch was running a small plant nursery in Hackney, but in 1771 he moved to St Petersburg in order to become head gardener to Catherine the Great's imperial Russian court. Another German émigré, Joachim Loddiges, acquired Busch's business and started a horticultural dynasty that by the early nineteenth century would become London's leading nursery.

The nursery covered land either side of Mare Street over the years it was active, including land where Hackney Town Hall is now located, but by 1816 it had settled on a site to the east of Mare Street as far as Elsdale Road, north to Paragon Street and south to Woolridge Way and Well Street. Its fame, as 'the Hackney Botanic Nursery Garden', had spread far beyond east London, and visitors from across Europe came to visit its glass houses and arboretum containing exotic species obtained from across the world, many of which were only available from Loddiges.

The nursery was particularly renowned for its innovative steam-heated hothouses, and one, the Grand Palm House, was described as the largest hothouse in the world, pre-dating anything at Kew by decades. It contained dozens of tropical plants, including palms, orchids and ferns from Africa, the Caribbean, South America and South Asia.

Along with the hothouses, Loddiges also pioneered the planting of an arboretum to show off the hardy plants they supplied. Of 3,075 listed in their 1830 catalogue, 1,000 were Roses. Over the years, Loddiges introduced many plants into cultivation in Britain and Europe for the first time. These include Wisteria, many Rhododendron and Azalea species, along with Hawthorns and Dogwoods from North America.

As we have seen, Loddiges were the principal supplier of the True Service Tree, and while we can speculate that the trees in Clapton Square may have come from just down the road, we cannot be sure. However, we do know that Loddiges supplied many stately homes, botanical gardens and cemeteries, including Abney Park in Stoke Newington, where some original Loddiges-supplied trees do still survive.

By the mid-nineteenth century Hackney was growing rapidly, and the demand for land was extremely high. Loddiges resided on land leased from St Thomas' Hospital, a lease that was set to expire in 1853. This effectively ended the Loddiges nursery, but a final hurrah was the transportation through the streets of London by 32 horses of one of the largest palm trees in the collection. A three-storeys-high Mauritius Fan Palm (which has subsequently been given the botanical name *Latania loddigesii*) left Hackney in 1854 for its new home in Sydenham at the relocated Crystal Palace.

Eleanor Road. On the corner, a paved build-out into the roadway has been planted with a pair of young white flowering **'Shirotae' Ornamental Cherries**. Stay on Eleanor Road as it forks to the left. This quiet street of substantial Victorian semis is lined with a fine array of interesting street trees, and some noteworthy front garden trees too. The first of these is a towering **Norway Maple** in the garden of the first Victorian house as the street curves round; there's a **Golden Rain Tree** and a **Medlar** elsewhere too.

The next tree to examine is a **Paper Mulberry** in the pavement on the eastern side next to an extensive hedge; this is followed by a pair of older cherry trees – early-flowering **'Accolade'** cultivars with delicate pale pink flowers. Beyond them is a deeper pink-flowering Magnolia, possibly **'Heaven Scent'**, while on the western side look out for more **Paper Mulberries** and

Paper Mulberry

White Mulberry

White Mulberries. A mulberry theme has started to emerge – and, rather wonderfully, a **Black Mulberry** has been planted to complete the set.

Mulberries are unusual: there are celebrated individual trees, often wizened and aged specimens, like the ones in the Temple (see page 204), but there are perhaps just 1,000 trees in the whole of the UK. Of these, the vast majority are black mulberries, the species producing wonderful juicy fruit in late summer, so to find black, white and paper mulberries within metres of one another is memorable. White mulberry is the species on which silkworms feed, while paper mulberry is not a true mulberry, but closely related.

At the end of Eleanor Road, turn right on Wilton Way, stopping briefly to look down Horton Road, where an unusual ornamental

Hybrid Peach can be seen. If you are following this route in March you may be rewarded with its head-turning fluorescent-pink blossom. Continue along Wilton Way as it goes under the railway. At the point where it is blocked to traffic, notice the Asian **Trident Maple** on your left, marking the point where you turn right on Hillman Street past the back of Art Deco Hackney Town Hall. A mature **Italian Alder** dominates, under whose towering canopy several different cherry varieties can be seen, including a **Winter Flowering Cherry** which will – confusingly – bloom right through the winter from November to April.

Follow the building round past a fine old **London Plane** tree into Reading Lane, passing a pair of **Common Lime** trees on your right. As you reach the front of the Town Hall, turn left again into the gardens between the building and Mare Street. The gardens consist of two formal lawns, each with a splendid **Canary Palm** at its centre. Planted sometime after the creation of the London Borough of Hackney in 1965, they are landmark trees that were perhaps planted as a memorial to Loddiges nursery which once occupied the same spot.

Pass through the gardens making for the iconic, and listed, Hackney Empire theatre. The Empire reflects the changing fortunes of its environs. It was designed in 1901 by the great theatre architect Frank Matcham to capitalise on Londoners' seemingly insatiable appetite for the entertainment spectacle of the moment: music hall. In its heyday it saw stars such as Marie Lloyd, Charlie Chaplin and Julie Andrews tread its boards. By the 1960s its fortunes

Canary Palm

Pheonix canariensis

One of only a handful of true palm trees that will grow outdoors in London, Canary Palms are the most frequent. Large examples can be seen in front gardens around the city, their original planters not realising perhaps how big they become: in almost no time at all Canary Palms will start sprouting leaves several metres long.

They originate, as the name suggests, from the Canary Islands, and are therefore used to a climate rather warmer than Londons. This does not appear to be a problem in Hackney, where frosts are increasingly rare, brief and mild.

Palm trees must be grown from seed, and are relatively slow-growing. Once established, they will develop attractive broad crowns consisting of huge, evergreen leaves or fronds. As the tree ages, it also gains height, the bottom leaves dying off as new leaves emerge, one at a time, from a central growing tip. Most London trees have barely left the ground, but Canary Palms can reach 20 metres or more. Our trees rarely flower, which could be down to their immaturity or possibly our climate being less than ideal.

But if the effects of global warming and the urban heat island remain unchecked, we might expect to see many more taller, fruit-bearing Canary Palms in the future.

The Hackney Empire

A Levantine **Judas Tree** marks the corner where Sylvester Path joins Sylvester Road. In early May this is a striking sight when it is resplendent with magenta blooms; at other times its attractive heart-shaped leaves and masses of seed pods covering the branches will give away its identity. Turn left briefly on Sylvester Road before turning right onto Marvin Street, just before the row of neatly pollarded **Common Limes** outside Graham Mansions. Marvin Street leads onto busy Graham Road, where you turn right until reaching the junction with Mare Street.

Cross Graham Road at the lights and continue north on Mare Street with the **Dawn Redwoods** in the central reservation behind you. Mare Street becomes Amhurst Road as it curves under the railway bridge, at the other side of which you will soon see the path leading up to Hackney Central station next to the former Victorian station building, now a bar.

had changed, and what was once a glamorous theatre had become a – very ornate – bingo hall. Fast forward to the 1990s, and it was a noted Alternative Comedy venue and, since a major renovation in the early 2000s, Hackney Empire now hosts a diverse programme including one of London's best pantos.

Now turn left back onto Wilton Way, following it around the back of the theatre. As the road turns left, you should continue straight on to Sylvester Path, passing, if you can resist, the Old Ship Inn. Previously known simply as the Ship, it has been here for over 200 years, witnessing many changes in Hackney. It is now a hip gastropub with a boutique hotel above.

Judas Tree flowers

London Fields

Called London Fields because of its location on the London side of the country village of Hackney, an open space has existed here for centuries and is recorded as 'London Field' as far back as 1560. Then, as for centuries before and afterwards, it was used as common grazing land, but by the mid-nineteenth century it was under threat from development as Hackney expanded. In 1860 it was saved from this fate and became a public park.

It was laid out with a series of avenues which are now shaded by mature London Plane trees. The signature feature of London Fields today, these are some of Hackney's oldest trees, and many are a distinct cultivar of Plane frequently seen in London's older parks.

Victorian nurserymen developed several forms of London Plane, each with specific features. Some are tall and relatively smooth-barked, others shorter with rougher trunks, while there are others with different leaf shapes, and even one with a very distinct short and very fat silhouette known as the 'Baobab' Plane, examples of which can be found in Wapping (see page 73) near Lincoln's Inn Fields (see page 196) and in Acton (see page 174).

London Fields' Planes are mostly of a form thought to be 'Palmata', a type recorded in the 1860s. But records were not always kept back then, suppliers were myriad, and Planes were the trees everyone wanted, so suppliers may have been tempted to send out whatever they could.

Researchers are gradually unpicking the story of London's Planes and the surprising number of different varieties to be found. In the meantime, the Pub on the Park is a great place to ponder the vagaries of Victorian tree planting, while admiring one of Hackney's finest green landscapes.

The Prospect of Whitby and Weeping Willow, Wapping

Docklands
Old and New

Wapping to Canary Wharf

We start in the cleaned-up and charming nineteenth-
century and end, just a few miles later, in a sanitised
twenty-first-century pastiche, passing through a part
of London utterly transformed twice over by successive
epochs in trade and commerce. The architectural contrasts
could not be more marked: in places the early stretches
(particularly the atmospheric pubs) are unchanged since
Dickens' time; its final section sees a skyline of glittering glass
towers still trying to outdo itself by soaring ever higher.
This is a walk characterised by, and alongside, water,
with some of the most sweeping, and sustained, panoramas
anywhere in the capital. And almost uniquely, its tree
planting – frequently riparian in character – is, with a couple
of exceptions, fascinatingly recent: when you start with a
blank canvas for your landscape, what do you plant. . . ?

Length: 4 miles (8,500 steps)
Start: Wapping Overground station
Finish: Canary Wharf (Jubilee Line)
Shortening: Limehouse (DLR and National Rail)
Accessibility: Pavements and level surfaces, crossing some busy roads, a few
unavoidable steps and narrow paths
Relative Difficulty: 2/5

1 – Wapping to King Edward Memorial Park

We start at Wapping Overground Station, and if you've arrived by train then the first marker for the extraordinary historical contrasts on this walk comes before you even head upstairs for the exit.

Go over to Platform 1 (northbound) and stand at the far end of it looking towards oncoming trains. As one rumbles into sight, illuminating the walls of the tunnel with its lights, you'll get a brief glimpse of its vaulted brick lining.

This section of the Overground, running under the Thames from Rotherhithe to Wapping, is the oldest underground railway line in London, constructed between 1823 and 1845 by the great Victorian engineer Isambard Kingdom Brunel. Initially the venture was a failure, and for some years

Captain Kidd pub and Wapping High Street

the tunnels were used as a kind of submarine shopping arcade; across the river at Rotherhithe there is a museum devoted to the project and Brunel (see page 109). Here you can descend into one of the original tunnel access shafts and visit the engine house used for pumping water during construction.

Outside the station, turn left on Wapping High Street, passing the Captain Kidd pub and the Metropolitan Police's Marine Unit, with your first stop the small Waterside Gardens on the left. These offer a first glimpse of the river, and also an opportunity to admire a small copse of silver-barked **Grey Poplars** with distinctive black diamond-shaped marks.

The architectural evidence of Wapping's dockland heritage is plain to see in Wapping High Street: the tall buildings flanking the narrow, still partially cobbled, street, now converted into luxury apartments, were riverside wharves for storing all the goods shipped ashore.

Back in the nineteenth century the street would have been straddled high up by metal walkways enabling access overhead from one warehouse to another, and cranes would have been hauling goods up and down onto and off horse-drawn carts. There is no truth in the claim, made frequently from the commentary on some of the tourist boats that ply the Thames, that 'WHARF' stands for 'WareHouse And River Frontage'.

Beyond the Waterside Gardens is an appropriately historic riverside pub, the Town of Ramsgate, from where, across the road, you enter St John's Churchyard. Like many small, old London churchyards, there's not much in the way of gravestones, but there are a few trees to admire, all **London Planes**. Of these the odd-looking, burry, multi-trunked tree on the right is of great interest. It is a **'Baobab'**, a rare cultivar characterised by a swollen bole and more deeply incised leaves than most London planes.

From the **'Baobab'** head over to the north-east corner gate leading to the church tower (all that remains of blitzed eighteenth-century St John's), admiring two huge planes elsewhere in the churchyard. Next to the church, the early eighteenth-century St John's School

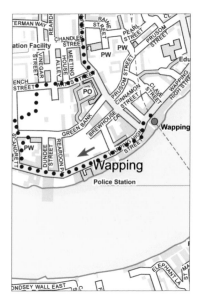

'Baobab' Plane in St John's Churchyard

building, adorned with quaint statues of schoolchildren, did survive the war. Our aim, though, is the Turk's Head (now a café), and the entrance to Wapping Gardens on Green Bank.

Wapping Gardens was originally laid out as Wapping Recreation Ground in 1886 following slum clearances. It is stuffed with mighty **London Planes** that have clearly appreciated this location not far from the river. Like those in Putney's Bishop's Park (see page 152), they are enormous and could easily be mistaken for eighteenth-century planting.

Cross over the Gardens to exit on Tench Street and turn right. After 50 metres, Tench Street becomes Watts Street and Turner's Old Star appears on the left. This Wapping institution overlooks Wapping Green, surrounded by **Horse Chestnuts**. Traverse the Green to arrive on Wapping

Grey Poplar bark

from Tower Bridge to the far side of the Isle of Dogs. This, quite simply, is why London became the pre-eminent mercantile city that it is: because the Thames could bring goods and trade from all over the world right to its heart.

In their heyday much of London's docks were grand affairs, as the former tobacco warehouse of Tobacco Dock shows. Its architect, Daniel Asher Alexander, also designed five magnificent warehouses immediately behind it alongside the former Western Dock; scandalously, they were demolished in the 1970s. Subsequently Rupert Murdoch's controversial News International printing works was built on the site, but has itself since made way for forest of apartment blocks.

Lane. Look out for a tree towards the back of the pocket park next to the Laksha Bay Indian restaurant: a curiosity in the shape of a **One-leaved Ash**, a cultivar of the common ash with confounding non-pinnate leaves. Turn left on Wapping Lane, and follow it up to Tobacco Dock, with its rusty-red replica galleon. We're now properly among what was, until the 1960s, the London Docks: one of the chain of docks that used to thread down the Thames, on both banks, all the way

In the 1990s Tobacco Dock enjoyed a brief and unsuccessful renaissance as a shopping mall, a self-styled Covent Garden of the East; the vast multi-storey car park opposite is testament to the scale of the folly. Now it's been restyled again as an events venue, its vast vaulted tunnels where, by the early 1800s, imported wines and

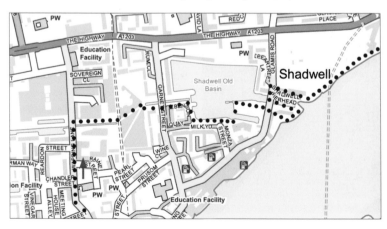

spirits were stored in temperature-controlled conditions, now a rather crepuscular workspace.

Opposite Tobacco Dock take the pleasantly bosky, paved path alongside the canal's southern edge, lined with sycamores and limes, and behind them rufous-barked **River Birches** in the garden of the apartment block on the right. Originally this canal linked St Katharine's Dock to the west with the London Dock all the way to its easternmost body of water, Shadwell Basin; nowadays it's no longer navigable and purely ornamental. After a couple of hundred yards we emerge into Wapping Woods.

Until 1969 you'd have been under water standing here: this was the Eastern Dock in the whole London Dock complex. Once drained and filled in, it was planted as this rectangle of parkland, with a tree population reflecting the tastes of the day. There are plenty of planes, and horse chestnuts, but you should look out for **White Willows** and more **Grey Poplars**, among which is an example of the very unusual columnar

Path from Tobacco Dock to Wapping Woods

River Birch

'**Tower**' cultivar. You may also wonder at the identity of the conifers dotted around: they are **Leyland Cypresses**, the source of 1980s suburban hedge-rage. It's not the most spectacular green space, but it could easily have been none at all.

Continue straight on across the crossroad of paths, following the sign to Shadwell Basin, and go under the red-painted metal bridge. As you emerge into the basin along an avenue of **Crack Willows**, ahead is your first view of the powerhouse skyline of Canary Wharf. To your left is the spire of St Paul's, Shadwell, and one of London's best postmodern housing developments. Maynards and Newlands Quays were built in the mid-1980s for the London Docklands

Docklands Redeveloped

Limehouse Basin in the 1980s

By the 1970s ever-larger ships, and particularly containerisation, had seen London's working docks decamp down river to deeper water at Tilbury. A numinous evocation of the windswept dereliction left behind can be had in *The Long Good Friday*, the classic 1980 gangster film starring Bob Hoskins and Helen Mirren.

A year later, therefore, Michael Heseltine, the then Secretary of State for the Environment, established the London Docklands Development Corporation (LDDC), a quango tasked with regenerating 8.5 square miles of the East End. There was no grand plan: indeed, precisely the opposite – had there been, argued its first chief executive, 'we would still be debating and nothing would have got built. Instead, we have gone for an organic, market-driven approach.'

The LDDC did finance a light railway to thread the whole area together, and a small airport to, it was hoped, fly in movers and shakers, but in its first years the market-driven approach had its critics: the little DLR was ridiculed as a toy-train set,

London City Airport and indeed the whole Canary Wharf development, built around the old West India Docks, got into financial difficulties, and office workers in the early days found themselves at lunchtime with little more than an Abbey National and a newsagent's.

But ultimately it did all work. From Tower Bridge all the way along the river and round the Isle of Dogs sweeps a ribbon of desirable residential property, albeit rather dwarfing the historic working-class communities that were already there. To take the pressure off the DLR the Jubilee Line had to be extended through Canary Wharf.

There is no other landscape in Britain remotely like it.

Development Corporation, and a fine example of the striking developments that sprung up around the former docklands from this time. Nowadays the basin, the only part of the old London Dock surviving as a tract of water, is the haunt of a few fishermen and cormorants, but there are plans to develop a lido here.

Follow the path (narrow in places, with one or two steps to negotiate) to the right around the edge of the basin, passing in the corner a newly planted small garden hosting a **Field Maple** and a **Wild Service Tree** and then, along the boundary of the basin, mature willows – an appropriately water-loving species – and **False Acacias**. Continue round the cobbled section and double back on yourself up the ramp and down again to leave the basin via the gateway by the big red bridge. This outsize Meccano construct, like its companion on the other side of the basin, is a bascule bridge: when the docks

Field Maple

were working it would swing up like Tower Bridge to allow vessels passage.

You've emerged onto Wapping Wall: turn right down to the Prospect of Whitby pub, one of London's most historic, that has outlived its spit-and-sawdust roots and these days is usually a haunt for tourist coaches. In homage to nearby Execution Dock, where, legend has it, pirates were frequently hanged, a replica scaffold has thoughtfully been erected on the foreshore

Shadwell Basin

Silver Limes, looking towards Rotherhithe

to prompt your reflections on nemesis and the transience of human existence as you wait for your scampi and chips. Visible over the wall is a luxuriant **Weeping Willow** in the pub garden.

Just before the Prospect, take the path between it and Trafalgar Court indicated by the circular Thames Path sign on the lamp post, past two **Ginkgo** trees, to come out on the river. The path bends round to the left, past four **Silver Lime** trees with benches beneath – a nice spot from which to take in your first full view of this mighty water-course, with Rotherhithe on the far bank (where the Ada Salter walk ends – see page 109) and, because the river meanders so sharply at this point, Canary Wharf apparently straight in front of you. The riverside path bends left opposite the Shadwell Basin Activity Centre. In early summer the **Judas Trees** overhanging the garden on the corner will be resplendent in magenta blossom.

Back at the red bridge turn right across it along Wapping Wall and, opposite

Pear Tree Lane, with another overhanging **Weeping Willow**, turn right down the path signposted 'Thames Path and King Edward VII Park'. This path, bordered further down by a column of dusty, gloomy **Leyland Cypresses**, takes you to a tranquil little riverside terrace. Watch out for bikes here, which for some reason are allowed along this section of the Thames Path and often under the misapprehension that it is a stage of the Tour de France.

The path winds round the handsome ventilation shaft for the Rotherhithe Tunnel and crosses the temporary driveway to the

Ginkgo leaves

huge construction site for the Thames Tideway project. Beneath this park is apparently one of the most polluting sewage overflows into the Thames, so currently a new shaft is being dug down to connect with the new super sewer being bored 60 metres beneath the Thames to take our effluent down to Beckton for treatment.

The coffer dam that encloses the sinking of this shaft will eventually reclaim a spur of land from the river to extend the park and its river frontage. In the meantime it's a noisy mess, and when construction began one of the melancholy first acts was the felling of the entire line of riverside trees that stood in its way.

King Edward Memorial Park was opened in 1922 in honour of the late monarch on the site of the former Shadwell Fish Market, and has a nice local feel, along with some surprising trees. Just where you turn

Fastigiate Golden Rain Tree in King Edward Memorial Park

Scarlet thorn

right beside the construction site along the bottom edge, there's a **'Beech Hill' Pear**, and lining the central avenue some old North American thorns, very difficult to positively identify, so a tentative ID of **Scarlet Thorn** is offered. In places trees have been replaced with younger **Broad-leaved Cockspur Thorn**. Elsewhere, the park's **Southern Catalpas** are noteworthy, along with some **Trees of Heaven**, a fine **Norway Maple** and, towards the north-east corner, a **Tulip Tree**, a young **Handkerchief Tree** and a **'Fastigiata' Golden Rain Tree**. Follow the turn-off to the right signposted Thames Path to take you out of the park through the gate and back on to the riverside.

2 – Free Trade Wharf to Limehouse

An even more sweeping panorama greets you, with the scintillating towers of Canary Wharf ahead in the distance like Shangri-La: that's where we're headed, and most of the way alongside the water. The further along the Thames Path you walk, the more the riverside view opens up behind you back towards Wapping and, beyond, a second clump of silver skyscrapers in the City of London, with the splinter of the Shard set apart to the south. Aside from the hills of south-east London or Parliament Hill in the north, this stretch of the river provides some of the most stunning prospects of the capital, especially on a bright, sunny day, or towards dusk when Canary Wharf's riverside towers burn gold in the setting sun.

Just beyond the vast redbrick semi-ziggurat of Free Trade Wharf and over a stepped pontoon bridge begins a long line of **White Poplars** – with their furry, ivory-backed leaves a very unusual and striking choice for this river frontage. Among them is a single, rare **Variegated Poplar**, which, it can only be assumed, slipped unnoticed into the consignment from the nursery. This row stretches all the way to Keepier Wharf, the apartment block that finally truncates it. They may be ruthlessly pollarded every year, presumably to preserve the river views for the flats behind, but one can only applaud such an imaginative arboreal choice. Behind them more **Judas Trees** provide colourful bloom in late spring.

Bear left and then right around Keepier Wharf, through its pretty little garden with a pair of **Cabbage Palms**, to emerge at the western end of Narrow Street. We'll explore this historic street shortly, but here we follow it up to the left to meet the thunder of traffic along the dual carriageway of the Highway. Cross *only* at the pelican crossing a few metres to the left, and go up Butcher Row, the road opposite. Halfway up Butcher Row cross over at another pelican crossing.

Before entering St James' Gardens we should note two other places of local interest. To the left is Cable Street, scene in 1930, towards its western end, of 'the Battle of Cable Street': the notorious confrontation between Oswald Mosley's Blackshirts and anti-Fascist demonstrators; it's commemorated a fair way up by a landmark mural on the wall of the old St George's town hall.

White Poplars on the Thames Path

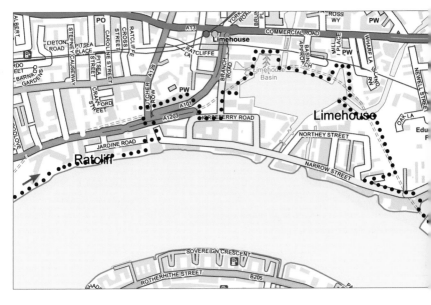

At its corner with Butcher Row there are a couple of **London Planes**, one of which is quite unusual in form. It is rather gaunt, with particularly fissured bark and deeply incised leaves: possibly it is an Oriental rather than London Plane.

Next to St James' Gardens is a handsome Georgian manor house, the former vicarage of St James', Ratcliff, the parish church that stood on this site until it was bombed during the war. Nowadays it is part of the Royal Foundation of St Katharine's, a religious retreat and conference centre whose bed and breakfast is reportedly of a high standard.

The Foundation's long history goes back to the twelfth century, when it was indeed situated at what is now St Katharine's Dock. England's archbishops have been known to gather here for secluded discussions, and occasionally you'll find yourself politely accosted at Limehouse DLR station by Polish nuns asking for directions. If you fancy a refreshment stop, just beyond the old vicarage is the Foundation's delightful Yurt café, situated in a surprisingly serene (given that the DLR rumbles almost overhead) pocket of green. Enjoy it while you can, though, because there are ominous plans to replace it with a tower block.

We're heading into St James' Gardens, though: another former churchyard turned pocket park running alongside the Rotherhithe Tunnel; both the path through it and the tunnel wall are lined with fine, mature **London Plane** trees – a comparatively rare sight on this walk – though those looking over the tunnel have recently undergone a real short back and sides to prevent boughs falling on the traffic below.

The path winds up and over the tunnel via a metal footbridge – again look out for

Pollarded Planes in St James' Gardens

Lycra-clad cyclists hurtling head-down heedlessly across – to the pinkish, postmodern western portal of the Limehouse Link Tunnel, built to speed traffic from the City underneath Canary Wharf and out onto the A13 and Essex-bound. At the time it was, mile for mile, the most expensive stretch of road ever built in Britain and, notwithstanding the little park, has created an unpleasant pollution hotspot at its Limehouse end. This road construction and new residential development have effectively obliterated the erstwhile neighbourhood of Ratcliff.

Descend via steps or ramp to Horseferry Road by the postbox and turn left, then left again up Branch Road. (If you want to save the second half of this walk for another day, continue up Branch Road to Limehouse DLR station at the top.) Cross over and a short distance up go across the cobbles between Berglen Court and Medland House to emerge on Limehouse Marina, another attractive body of water, with the tower of Hawksmoor's St Anne's

church visible beyond.

In the nineteenth century this was Limehouse Dock, opened in 1820 to connect the Regent's Canal (which joins it in its north-eastern corner) with the Thames, and mainly used to trans-ship cargoes from Thames vessels onto barges to go up the canal, which winds round London all the way to

Regent's Canal at Limehouse Basin

Little Venice and meets the Grand Union Canal coming down from the north. It's since been developed as an increasingly popular marina for both upmarket houseboats and the odd millionaire's private yacht..

We're going to follow the marina all the way round, clockwise, past the DLR railway viaduct (another historical relic: the oldest surviving railway viaduct in the world) and a row of **Ash** trees, over the canal by the gunmetal-grey footbridge, and round to the right past the dental practice, all the way to a display board on the wildlife of Docklands – you can see the odd tern swooping onto the water here in summer, and a small flock of red-crested pochards sometimes visits, but for kingfishers you'll have to follow the Regent's Canal up towards Victoria Park.

At the display board cross the black metal footbridge by a pair of small **Irish Yews** and, down the other side, double back behind you to follow the Limehouse Cut towpath round for 50 metres, until you turn right at the curved grey-brick wall

(signposted 'Thames Path, Historic Pubs – we'll come to that) to enter Ropemakers' Fields, another neat little park, always well used by locals. The circular lawn at the top is bordered by **Turkish Hazels**, the central path an avenue of **Horse Chestnuts**, and its boundary back on Narrow Street is demarcated by **Limes**.

Turning right down the chestnut avenue, branch off right at the bandstand to exit the park through the gate. The tall, thin building to your right, the sole example of any antiquity on this north side of Narrow Street, used to be a pub called The House They Left Behind: everything else around it was flattened by the Luftwaffe.

We find ourselves beside a copse of mature **Southern Catalpas**, quite magnificent in white summer bloom, and, just ahead on the south side of the street, at the end of a terrace of tall Georgian houses, the historic Grapes pub. Singular, mind, because this is now the only historic pub left on Narrow Street, and really should get your patronage.

Ropemakers' Fields

Narrow Street

Narrow Street is the last vestige of old riverside London between Wapping and Canary Wharf, and has hosted a raft of literary, political and mercantile life.

Sailing barges with the Grapes beyond, early 1900s

Arguably, life in Narrow Street is focused on the Grapes, Dickens's model for the Six Jolly Fellowship Porters in *Our Mutual Friend* and still laudably unmodernised. Nowadays it's owned, inter alia, by Sir Ian McKellen.

Under McKellen the Grapes continues to make its own history: in the early days diary columns would report sightings at the bar of celebs like Kristin Scott-Thomas, while Stephen Fry and David Cameron are said to have dined there to discuss LGBT rights. Venture out onto the balcony at the back for a particularly up-close prospect of the Thames and the somewhat predictable Antony Gormley figure from his *Another Time* series McKellen got permission to plant on the foreshore.

Another Narrow Street resident, the *Times* columnist Matthew Parris, made more esoteric history by fulfilling a long-held ambition to swim across the Thames. The plan was to swim from Globe Wharf on the south bank to Ratcliff Cross Steps at the end of Narrow Street, but when Parris consulted the tide tables he got his calculations out by an hour. Finding himself being carried steadily upstream, he had to climb ashore at the King Edward VII Park and run back down the Highway in the early hours with his pants full of mud. (*Do not try this*: swimming in this part of the Thames is now officially forbidden.)

For a fascinating evocation of life along it track down a copy of *Limehouse Lil* by Rozelle Raynes, who until a few years ago lived at number 88: as late as the 1960s the river here was thick with sailing barges (Barge Wharf, now a private residence with an arched frontage, was the headquarters of the company that ran them), and Narrow Street an almost exclusively working-class area and even, if you weren't from these parts, a little dodgy.

3 – Narrow Street to Canary Wharf

*Southen Catalpas
on Narrow Street
frame the Grapes*

We now turn left along Narrow Street past the catalpas and a solitary **American Sweetgum**, crossing over at Dunbar Wharf. The name now graces a large block of luxury flats, but beyond it the preserved nineteenth-century building was once the wharf of the eponymous Duncan Dunbar, who ran a shipping line from here conveying convicts to Australia and troops to the Crimean War. We go underneath a large opening in the modern block, signposted 'Cyclists Dismount' (look up in summer to see the house martins' nests, stippled spheres of mud, wedged into the interstices of the concrete overhang), and over a metal footbridge to reach the river front again.

Now, as you follow the Thames Path along towards the Thames Clipper's Canary Wharf jetty, you have the best views back up the Thames towards the city, and its increasingly high-rise skyline panning all the way from Nine Elms to the cluster of Cheesegrater, Gherkin and Pinnacle. A line of pollarded **London Planes** is succeeded by

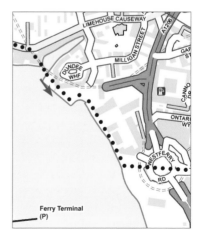

Pin Oaks on the Thames Path towards Canary Wharf

a column of conical **Pin Oaks**, their leaves turning an attractive yellow in late summer and darkening to a wine hue in autumn, all the way along the promenade to the Thames Clipper jetty. Someone could have decided to just chuck in a load of Chanticleer Pears, if anything, but once again the tree planting has added striking colour and definition to a still youthful landscape. The whole thing looks meant to be.

Ascend the steep steps (there is a lift as well) opposite the Clipper station, cross at the pelican crossing and enter Westferry Circus gardens, a small suntrap densely planted around its perimeter with everything from a **Southern Magnolia**, a **Persian Ironwood** and **Red Oaks** to a **Dawn Redwood**, with even an **English Oak** making an appearance. Exit the garden on its far side, cross another pelican crossing,

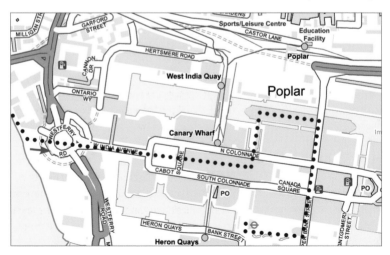

and head straight along the main avenue towards Cabot Square.

The tree planting along here could not be more traditional (in keeping with the faux-classical tenor of much of this early North American-inspired Canary Wharf architecture): an outer avenue of limes; an inner of **London Planes**. At the end go up the few steps into Cabot Square with its fountain: even more respectfully formal planting here: pleached **Silver Limes** all around, no less, as though we're at Hampton Court or even Versailles!

Now we really are in exclusively (post) modern London: Canary Wharf. Once this too was more docks – primarily the West India Docks (some of whose imposing warehouses survive as the Museum of London Docklands, a fascinating exhibition, and free entry), where sugar and spice arrived from the Caribbean plantations.

We have two more spectacularly unlikely plantations to view, so head inside

West India Avenue

Plants and People

That London is as arboreally diverse as it is, is partly thanks to its status as a port. Ever since the Romans first settled Londinium 2,000 years ago, London's docks have been the point of entry for people, animals and plants from all over the world.

With the Romans came Mulberries and Sweet Chestnuts, and since then innumerable plants – for food, industry and out of mere curiosity – have turned up on these shores. The invention of the Wardian Case – a kind of terrarium – in the nineteenth century, meant live plants could be easily shipped all over the world and between very different environments. London's docks must have witnessed tens of thousands of Wardian Cases arriving, leaving or in transit.

All the while, however, plants have also arrived incognito. From Trees of Heaven to Sycamores and Turkish Hazel, you only need look in any unkempt corner of London to see vegetation, including trees, from all corners of the world making this city home.

Gilbey's wine barrels at Western Dock, Wapping, 1907

HSBC Tower from the Roof Garden

the shopping mall (yes, really). Bear in mind that Canary Wharf is a 'privately owned public space', and not an unreservedly public space – but this is also the way to the DLR station. Proceed straight ahead, through the station concourse and out the other side, across the rotunda (a choice of chain coffees and cakes here if you wish), and on down the central arcade, until you reach an intersection by a set of cash machines.

Turn left here, and keep going through the swing doors until you come out into the open again, straight across the rather windy piazza to a very long covered walkway ahead, leading to the Crossrail station. The trains here, when they finally arrive years late, will run 30 metres underground, but we're going to take the escalators up to the top of the building, following the signs to the Roof Garden.

You emerge beneath a state-of-the-art 'biome': a translucent conservatory that symbolises the hyper-reality of the entire Canary Wharf estate. It could be a backdrop from a near-future sci-fi movie. Everything is enclosed in a constantly surveilled, corporately controlled and pristine environment; interpretation panels explain that the inspiration came from the Wardian Case, a glass terrarium used by nineteenth-century plant hunters to transport their finds over long distances at sea.

Defying logic, this bizarre, sub-tropical garden offers a parody of sanctuary three floors up above layers of enterprise and entertainment. Plants from all corners of the temperate world are here, echoing the global reach of London's new financial hub, and rooted not in London's rubble-filled

earth, but in some unspecific aerial habitat that could equally be Dubai, Chicago, Seoul or Moscow.

But there are some interesting specimens among these ground-lit walkways. Look out for three species of antipodean tree ferns: **Golden** and **New Zealand Tree Ferns** and the **Australian Soft Tree Fern**. They rub shoulders with several bamboos and magnolias, some **Japanese Maples**, **American Sweetgums** and at least one **Persian Silk Tree**.

At the far end take the lift or escalators down to the ground level once more and exit onto Upper Bank Street, which you should follow as it passes the HSBC and Citibank towers until you reach an entrance to Ca-

Roof Garden Tree Ferns

Dawn Redwoods on Reuters Plaza

nary Wharf Tube station on your right. Take the entrance to Jubilee Park just beyond it.

This is another magnificent creation: an entire **Dawn Redwood** forest (interspersed with a few **Swamp Cypresses**), in summer a magnificent sight with the almost pea-green foliage shimmering in the breeze, and another towering species to complement the buildings powering up all around. Wandering through the redwoods is as unreal as the roof garden, but not unpleasant, as water features, lunch nooks for office workers and grassy glades open up. At the other side, you emerge on the piazza in front of the western

entrance to Canary Wharf Station.

Just as you began this walk by arriving by train in the nineteenth century, at Brunel's station with its narrow platforms, brick-vaulted tunnels and twisty spiral staircase, so you should end it by taking the Jubilee Line home, and descending into Norman Foster's truly awesome station. From the imposing proscenium arch of the entrance long escalators glide you down into a vast concrete cavern – vaulted too, but on a sweeping scale. This is only the ticket hall: the platforms are on another hushed concourse a further escalator ride down. . .

Dawn Redwood

Metasequoia glyptostroboides

Dawn Redwoods are one of the select group of deciduous conifers and, remarkably, they've only been with us for 70 years, but in the space of a few decades, they've made a big impact.

Of course, they've actually been around for millions of years, but they've only been in the UK since the late 1940s. Fossil records were described and named by a Japanese scientist in 1941 as 'Metasequoia', meaning 'like a *Sequoia*' (for the uninitiated, *Sequoia* is a genus containing one species, the Giant Redwood).

So it was big news when, a couple of years later, rumours started circulating about a new conifer discovered in a remote corner of China. After the Second World War, Chinese scientists set out to look for this tree, and found a few specimens thriving in the forests of Hubei province.

With scientific interest reaching fever pitch, in 1947 seeds were sent to Boston's Arnold Arboretum, who promptly distributed some to other scientific institutions around the world including Kew. From these seeds, saplings were raised and, once the media got wind, the world was briefly awed by the discovery of a 'living fossil'. It helped that the living fossil was a large, attractive and fast-growing tree.

As a result of all the interest in this new 'discovery', plants were in demand for parks and gardens everywhere. By the turn of the millennium Dawn Redwood was frequently the choice for a self-respecting new development wanting to make a statement, and increasingly used for street planting.

Jubilee Park Dawn Redwoods

In London these days you are never far from a Dawn Redwood, and many fine examples can be seen on walks in this book, including those behind the High Court in Holborn (see page 198), and down the central reservation of Mare Street in Hackney (see page 52). But perhaps the most impressive are the hundreds that form a plantation in the heart of Canary Wharf.

Caucasian Wingnut on Wilson Grove

Ada Salter and the
Beautification of Bermondsey

Borough to Rotherhithe

Bermondsey and Rotherhithe stretch along the south bank
of the Thames east of Tower Bridge. Historically an area of
docks, warehouses, food processing factories and tanneries,
in the nineteenth and early-twentieth centuries it was home
to tens of thousands living in insanitary, disease-ridden slums.

In 1897 an idealistic young woman arrived in
what was one of London's poorest districts determined to
transform it, along with the lives of its people. Key to her
vision was the beautification of the borough through
a pioneering environmental programme, including the
planting of thousands of trees, of which one species –
the Tree of Heaven – stands out.

This route traces the former Borough of Bermondsey
through its trees, the legacy of Ada Salter, later to become
its mayor, and the green socialist utopia she helped create.

Length: 5.5 miles (11,000 steps)
Start: Borough Tube station (Northern Line)
Finish: Rotherhithe Overground station
Shortening: Bermondsey Tube station (Jubilee Line)
Accessibility: Pavements and level surfaces, crossing some busy roads and a park.
Steps into Hamilton Square can be avoided.
Relative Difficulty: 2/5

1 – Borough to the Alfred Salter Playground

The classical eighteenth-century Borough church St George the Martyr lies diagonally opposite the Tube station, and is the conspicuous landmark you should head for.

Next to it is a paved area forming the corner of Great Dover Street and Long Lane, now planted with an intriguing selection of trees. The side joining Long Lane hosts four March-flowering **'Merrill' Magnolias**, a splendid sight when they are covered in white blooms. Joining them are a pair of **Dawn Redwoods** and two small, densely canopied trees hugging the church wall. These are unusual **'Nana' Southern Catalpas**, a slow-growing cultivar planted for their compact form rather than the blowsy flowers normally associated with the species.

Skirt round the church to its northern side and admire the **Ginkgos** planted in what was, until just a few years ago, Tabard Street. A turning off Borough High Street, Tabard Street was constructed around 1750,

cutting through St George's churchyard and dislocating it from the marooned church. The churchyard is still here, and a towering **London Plane** marks a gap in the buildings opposite the church. Head through the iron gates and into this walled sanctuary. It is now a formal garden with old headstones moved to its periphery.

Make for the doorway in the north wall, noting the mature **Sycamore** to the right. Mounted on the brick wall is a panel identifying the wall as formerly that of the Marshalsea, the debtors' prison where in 1824 Charles Dickens's father was incarcerated. As a result, 12-year-old Charles was forced to work in a blacking factory (producing shoe polish) to bring in money for the family. The poor, industrial areas around these parts feature in many of Dickens's novels,

'Nana' Southern Catalpas at Borough

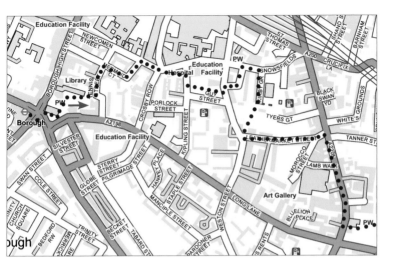

and the Marshalsea in particular provides the backdrop for *Little Dorrit*.

Through the wall, turn right on Angel Place, and then left on Tennis Street, with the Tabard Gardens Estate on your right. A purple-leaved **'Crimson King' Norway Maple** in the estate gardens marks the corner with Mermaid Court and a right turn. Follow the road round to the left as it becomes Bowling Green Place and, just after a finely shaped **False Acacia**, turn right into Newcomen Street. Traverse Crosby Place opposite the entrance to Guy's Hospital and a newly planted row of **Field Maples**.

Continue for a few metres to a path on your right just before a row of shops. Optionally, take the path into Hamilton Square, or continue on Snowsfields past the shops and the Miller pub, turning right into Kipling Street. If you have taken the path into Hamilton Square (which has some steps to navigate) where it forks, keep left with the service road below on your left and emerge

on Kipling Street. While on the path, note the tree in the pub's backyard, a **Tree of Heaven**. It appears to have seeded itself rather too closely to the wall, which is now beginning to crack as the tree rapidly expands in all directions.

Sycamore and Marshalsea wall

Ada Salter

Ada and Alfred Salter, spades in hand, planting a Tree of Heaven

Ada Brown was born in Northamptonshire in 1866 and arrived in London, to administer to the poor and needy, some thirty years later. She married Dr Alfred Salter in 1900, having converted him to her Quaker beliefs, Alfred was to later become MP for Bermondsey.

By all accounts theirs was a marriage built around debate, mutual support and deeply-held convictions. Ada insisted on living in the slums alongside the people she was determined to help, arguably a decision that caused the greatest tragedy in their lives, the death of their only daughter, Joyce, from scarlet fever aged just eight. Alfred was clever, principled but obstinate, while Ada was open, thoughtful and diplomatic, and together they made their mark on Bermondsey.

When Ada Salter became Mayor of Bermondsey in 1922, she was the first woman to be elected mayor in London, and the first female Labour mayor anywhere in the UK. She had been a Bermondsey councillor on and off since 1909 (since before women were able to vote), and had already begun to make her mark on Bermondsey. By 1920 she had set up the Beautification Committee, with the intention of improving the environment, and by extension the lives of Bermondsey's residents.

The Committee went on to plant 9,000 trees around the streets, parks and estates of the borough, and by the 1930s had beautified every possible corner and instituted a campaign to promote window-box gardening across the new estates too. Ada had a particular penchant for the Tree of Heaven, which she planted in such quantities that it gave the borough a distinct arboreal character. While they are relatively short-lived, Trees of Heaven planted by the borough council over several decades can still be seen, ageing gracefully, defining Bermondsey as much as the model housing of Wilson Grove or estates like St John's or Neckinger.

Of course, it wasn't just Trees of Heaven that were planted. Many more planes and poplars went in, and the Planes in particular are just beginning to hit early maturity on streets like Tower Bridge Road. The poplars have not fared so well, and many have disappeared, but, like those on the corner of Grange Walk, some giants are still around.

Bermondsey was not the first or last place to plant Trees of Heaven – they can be seen all over London – but because of the quantity planted here, and the convictions that led to their planting, they have become synonymous with Ada Salter and the beautification of Bermondsey.

Tree of Heaven outside the Miller pub

Bermondsey on Booth's Poverty Map

On Kipling Street, glance back at the mature, planted **Tree of Heaven** on the corner, the likely progenitor of the rogue pub garden tree. You have just entered the former borough of Bermondsey, and that tree on the corner might be regarded as a boundary tree. Before 1965, the land to the north and west was in the old borough of Southwark, which covered a much smaller area than today's super-borough.

The boundary tree is fairly elderly for its species, possibly 60 years old, about as old as the pub it stands next to. As it is a Tree of Heaven, it has a direct connection to the trees planted by Mayor Ada Salter's Beautification Committee.

Cross Kipling Street to enter Guy Street Park, a small green patch dotted with magnificent **London Planes**. The park is in

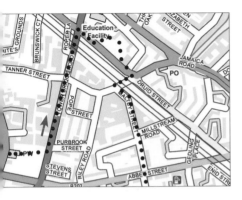

two halves: all the mature trees belong to the western part, a row of them separating it from the more formal eastern part, which was added after the Second World War. Industrial Bermondsey suffered badly during the war, and in the decades afterwards new parks and gardens were laid out where bombed-out houses, factories and warehouses were demolished.

Leave Guy Street Park on Weston Street, turn left and, almost immediately, cross the road and head down an unmarked alleyway – Ship and Mermaid Row – between two former warehouse buildings. This narrow, cobbled thoroughfare gives an impression of stepping back in time, only the double yellow lines reminding us that we are still in the modern metropolis.

Follow it round as it turns left along an old brick wall with a **London Plane** tree hanging over it halfway along. As you draw level, the plane is quite a sight. Sandwiched between the wall and a fence, it appears to have been boxed in for a century or more. Could it pre-date the 1897 Guinness Trust Estate next to it?

At the end of Ship and Mermaid Row you are greeted back on Snowsfields by a pair of **Nettle Trees**. So-called for their nettle-shaped leaves, they originate from southern Europe and are beginning to appear more frequently in some parts of London. Their tolerance for drought and heat mean they are well suited to dealing with our city's warming climate. Turn right here, passing the ornate, collonaded entrance to the Guinness Trust Estate. Just after this, turn right onto Kirby Grove, with a distinctly leaning **Strawberry Tree** marking the corner of Melior Place behind you.

Himalayan Birch-lined Kirby Grove leads past the woodland garden of Snows-fields School on your left, and enters Leath-ermarket Gardens next to Bermondsey Village Hall. The gardens are another open space originating from the destruction of the Second World War. in decades past, this area was the heart of Bermondsey's tanning industry – indeed, the nineteenth-century London Leather, Hide and Wool Exchange can be seen just across Leathermarket Street on the south side of the Gardens.

Strawberry Tree fruit

Leather tanning was a particularly noxious industry, and no doubt extremely unpleasant to live next door to. The famous *London Poverty Map* drawn up by the Victorian social reformer Charles Booth shows a concentration in Bermondsey, where multitudes were crammed into squalid living conditions between tanneries, warehouses, food processing factories and riverside wharves.

Leave Leathermarket Gardens past the **'Crimson King' Norway Maple** in its southeast corner, and turn left onto Leathermarket Street, passing a series of Victorian warehouses, including the Morocco Store forming the corner with Morocco Street, a name recalling an important source of leather imports. At the end of Leathermarket Street, turn right into trendy Bermondsey Street.

Not far down this now-gentrified street, you pass Tanner Street Park on the left, with a young **Austrian Pine**, a **Turkish Hazel** and a group of white-flowered **Wild Cherries** enticing pedestrians off the street. Continue past the White Cube gallery to the right, with its well-clipped **Holm Oak** on the corner with Lamb Walk, until you reach the Portmeirion Gothic of St Mary Magdalen Church. Enter the churchyard via a gate in the black iron railings flanked by a pair of Trees of Heaven.

There are several interesting trees here, most notably a pair of mature **Ginkgos** at the rear of the church. Look out too for a weeping **'Pendula' Ash** and a **Box Elder** as you make your way to the north-east corner and a gate onto Tower Bridge Road. Turn left as you exit and head north under the Bermondsey Borough Council-planted **London**

Holm Oak outside White Cube

Plane canopy for about 300 metres, taking the first right immediately after the railway bridge onto Druid Street. Continue past the low-rise flats and their attendant **Chanticleer Pear** trees, taking the next left on a wide, bollard-blocked path, and immediately turn right into the Alfred Salter Playground.

Alfred Salter, and more so his wife Ada, were instrumental in the transformation of Bermondsey during the early twentieth century, turning it from an insanitary industrial slum into something akin to a garden suburb. The playground is now part of the St John's Estate, typical of the modern homes Bermondsey Council built under the leadership of Mayor Ada Salter. The playground is unremarkable, save for a raised bed on which a fine **Tree of Heaven** is growing. As a plaque explains, this memorial tree, perhaps just 20 years old, marks the spot where the Salters' ashes are interred.

Bermondsey's Leather Industry

Former London Leather, Hide & Wool Exchange

For centuries, Bermondsey had been the centre of London's leather trade, an industry reliant on a plentiful supply of animal skins, oak bark, various unsavoury chemicals and water. Its proximity to a large market and riverborne transportation also helped, and by 1792 a third of the leather produced in the country came from Bermondsey.

With Smithfield meat market only a mile or two away on the northern edge of the City of London, animal skins were readily available, but to turn these into leather requires a series of laborious, smelly and even hazardous processes. All the various stages of leather production, and its allied trades like warehousing and exporting, were carried out in Bermondsey, particularly around Long Lane and Bermondsey Street.

Before an animal skin can be tanned, it must have any hair and fat removed, in a process known as 'felling', using lime and other chemicals. Next it may be 'bated': a particularly noxious process to soften it, involving urine and dung. The resulting rawhide is then ready for tanning, another chemical process which uses large quantities of oak bark.

If you have already followed the North London Ancient Woodland walk on page 10, you will have seen some fine oak trees growing as standards among the coppice. Every time one of these was felled, its bark would most likely have ended up in Bermondsey. Indeed, a whole trade arose around the process of stripping bark from trees, remembered in the family name 'Barker'.

In the woodlands of south London, such as those around Abbey Wood, there is evidence of oak trees being coppiced, a practice which would result in a more reliable flow of oak bark. Of course, Bermondsey was not far from the Great North Wood, a swathe of woodland that once stretched from Croydon to New Cross, and no doubt another source of oak bark.

2 – Druid Street to St James' Church

Leave the playground at its eastern end and turn left on Druid Street for a short while before turning right on Tanner Street under the railway viaduct. Once through the arches, turn left almost immediately on Maltby Street, marked by a young **Hornbeam**. The Victorian railway arches here and the Ropewalk just beyond have been transformed into a gastro hotspot rivalling Borough Market (but without quite so many tourists). It's an ideal refreshment stop, as well as a great place to stock up on foodie provisions.

Continue on Maltby Street under well-established **Norway Maples** until you reach Plane-lined Abbey Street, which you should turn briefly right onto. Cross at the lights and then double back to turn right

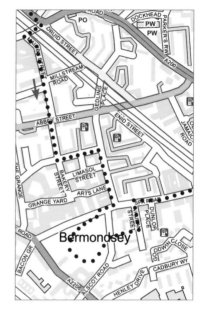

again into the continuation of Maltby Street. A little way down, a row of trees line up against an incongruous brick wall: a trio of **Chinese Tree Privets** flanked by a pair of '**Fastigiata' Hornbeams**.

At the junction ahead, turn left onto Grange Walk. Make for the pair of huge billowing **Poplars** in the distance. These trees, well pollarded over the years, are likely veterans of the Beautification Committee – as well as Trees of Heaven. There are many different poplar species, hybrids and cultivars, notoriously difficult to tell apart, but those planted in the twentieth century were often Hybrid Black Poplars: these probably are too.

The poplars mark the junction of Neckinger, a street named for the Thames

Hybrid Black Poplar

Entrance to the Neckinger Estate

tributary that is now culverted and runs under the road. Ahead of you is the modernist Neckinger Estate with its distinctive archway. Built in 1938 by Bermondsey Borough Council, the flats are typical of the new housing constructed to replace the slums. They occupy a site that was once a tannery.

Turn right on Neckinger towards Spa Road and Bermondsey's old civic centre and, opposite the Queen's Arms, turn right, with the neoclassical Bermondsey Town Hall building on your right (these days, rather upmarket apartments). Opposite this building, cross to enter Bermondsey Spa Gardens. Back in the eighteenth century, people flocked here to take the restorative waters, but all trace of a spa has long since disappeared. By the nineteenth century, houses occupied the area now covered by the gardens. They were badly bombed during the war, and the park was opened in 1952.

In the park, turn right on the circular track until, roughly opposite the former

Bermondsey Central Library, an ornate brick building and now a Buddhist Centre, look out for a young **Tree of Heaven**. Like the tree in the Alfred Salter Playground, it is a memorial tree planted, according to the nearby plaque, to remember 'the Bermondsey Councillors of old who lined the streets with the Tree of Heaven to ease the effects of poverty on health and the quality of life'.

Now make your way round the park, admiring the specimen trees within, including more splendid old **Hybrid Poplars** and a couple of variegated **'Drummondii' Norway Maples**, to leave in the south-east corner onto Alscot Road. Almost opposite is a path between a children's playground and a car park leading to another mid-century Bermondsey housing estate. Turn left in front of the flats, and then go through the gap between the two blocks into a central square and Vauban Street. Notable here are several very stout and elderly **Trees of Heaven**, which have also been much pollarded – a treatment that does not suit this species.

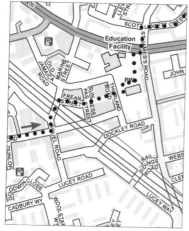

Passage on your right, both turnings lined with **Honey Locusts**, to continue through the new flats on Frean Street, passing more Judas Trees before you arrive on Thurland Road with St James' Church in front of you. As with the Long Lane burial ground, Mayor Salter's Bermondsey Borough Council set about moving the headstones and turning the former St James' churchyard into a children's play area and flower garden. Now, the grounds are a somewhat sedate park, where you can see several **Silver Birches**, a fine **Sycamore** and, inevitably, **Trees of Heaven**.

Turn left on Vauban Street and then right onto Spa Road past a newly planted **Oriental Plane**. Continue along Spa Road until you reach Rouel Road on the left. Turn left past a newly planted **American Sweetgum** opposite some more butchered **Trees of Heaven**. As the street curves round to become Enid Road, turn left under the railway on Marine Street by a **Southern Magnolia**, pausing to admire an unmolested **Tree of Heaven** beyond to your left, set off by the Shard behind in the distance.

Just before Marine Street emerges on the other side of the railway viaduct, turn right on Frean Street, a name that recalls the once-famous Peek Frean biscuit works in Bermondsey, from which emanated rather more pleasant aromas than those from the tanning industries. On your left a huge **Norway Maple** spreads over the street from an adjacent office car park and, as you continue along, note the **Judas Trees**, which in May are resplendent with magenta blossom. Pass Ness Street on your left and Sun

Tree of Heaven on Enid Street

Tree of Heaven

Ailanthus atissima

Trees of Heaven are named for their towering stature and rapid, heaven-ward growth: they can reach 20 metres or more in just 60 years. They are handsome too: soaring branches form a domed canopy bedecked with large, distinctive leaves complemented in late summer by reddish seed bunches.

Ripening Tree of Heaven seeds

urban environments. They can poison competing plants, and male trees produce flowers that can be nauseatingly pungent. The habit which alarms many, however, is their propensity for reproduction. Both through seeds and suckers, Trees of Heaven like to make their presence felt, and will rapidly colonise any available ground. Part of the fun of finding a mature Tree of Heaven is looking for its offspring, which are rarely far away and, given their propensity for rapid growth, can appear to be purposefully planted.

As well as being Ada Salter's favourite tree, Trees of Heaven have another Bermondsey connection. The species arrived in Britain from China in 1751, imported by the noted plant dealer Peter Collinson. Collinson, like Salter and her husband, was a Quaker, and on his death in 1768 his remains were interred in the Society of Friends burial ground on Long Lane. During Ada's reign in Bermondsey, very little land was available in what was one of London's most densely populated boroughs. As a result, graveyards were transformed into play areas, and the Long Lane burial ground, which had stopped being used for that purpose in 1855, was transformed into the Long Lane Children's Playground.

Particularly on younger trees, the pinnate leaves can be enormous – up to a metre long – and the young plants have a similar capacity for enormous growth. Trees can grow to four or five metres in as many years, making them appear well-established in a very short time. In many ways they are the ideal tree to plant if quick results are required; a fact not lost on politicians ...

But these wonder trees have some downsides too. They live fast and die young: 70 years is a good innings, less in unnatural

3 – Wilson Grove to Rotherhithe

Leave St James' by the exit in the north-east corner, arriving next to the mock-Tudor Gregorian pub. In front of the pub, steps lead down to a subway under the busy Jamaica Road, which emerges on Bevington Street in the post-war Dickens Estate.

Silver Maples have been planted here, including many with deeply incised leaves, possibly the 'Wieri' cultivar. Turn right off Bevington Street on Scott Lidgett Crescent, marked by a low, very broad-canopied Norway Maple. The street is named after a Wesleyan minister, John Scott Lidgett, who founded the Bermondsey Settlement where Ada and Alfred first met in 1898. The Settlement was rather like a mission, where people – often young Christians committed to social change – would live and carry out improving work within the community.

Scott Lidgett Crescent becomes Janeway Street and low-rise houses with gardens around them. Turn right here past

'Weiri' Silver Maple leaves

a False Acacia, some Silver Birches and a couple of old Hollies, before being deposited in tree-lined Wilson Grove, with a Caucasian Wingnut straight ahead. With their model housing, these streets represent

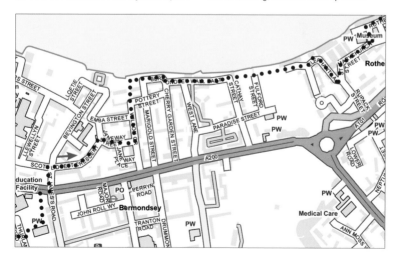

Model housing on Wilson Grove

Ada Salter's vision for the transformation of Bermondsey into a garden village. Constructed in the late 1920s, they replaced overcrowded slums, but, while Ada wanted to build more like them, available space and finances contrived to ensure that most new housing in Bermondsey was to be flats.

Originally, Wilson Grove was planted with Silver Birches, a species popular for urban planting at the time. Its delicate pendulous habit was very much in keeping with Art Deco design sensibilities but, like the Tree of Heaven, it is a rather short-lived tree. However that did not stop them being replaced in the intervening decades with Trees of Heaven.

As we have seen, this species grows rapidly, and by 1987 some were large enough to succumb in October to the Great Storm , a weather event that toppled thousands of mature trees across London. Wilson Grove's lost trees were replaced

with Caucasian Wingnuts, which now seems like a strange choice, or perhaps simply a mistake. Wingnuts have very similar large, pinnate leaves to Trees of Heaven, and in the vast clean-up and replanting operation, could it be that, somewhere between or-

Wilson Grove shortly after construction

Turkish Hazels on Bermondsey Wall East

dering and supplying, a similar-looking but completely unrelated species was installed?

In little over 30 years the Wingnuts – a huge, spreading species – have grown rapidly. So much so that they have started to buckle the pavements, and grown such prodigious girths that getting past them can be challenging, especially for those with wheelchairs or pushchairs.

Turn left on Wilson Grove towards the river. At the end, turn right on Bermondsey Wall East where, from the riverside gardens, excellent views of the Thames up to Tower Bridge can be had. Walk through a **Turkish Hazel** avenue until you briefly re-join the road at the junction with Cherry Garden Street (a euphemistic name remembering its association with prostitution in centuries past, rather than the ornamental cherry trees now lining this street). Continue east along Bermondsey Wall East, passing another opening in the buildings to the river, before you arrive at an open area, with the river on your left and a grassy area to your right containing a few ruined remains of a fourteenth-century Royal residence.

The Terrace on your left acts both as an impromptu beer garden for the popular and highly recommended Angel pub, and as the setting for a series of cast bronze statues. What they lack in artistic excellence they make up for with historic and social importance, portraying the entire Salter family, the cat, Alfred, Ada and their daughter Joyce. It is particularly fitting that the figure of Ada has a spade in her hand.

Beyond the Angel, keep hugging the river, where the riverside road becomes a path through King's Stairs Gardens, a small landscaped park with some old planes and, on the left just after a particularly narrow building, three **Caucasian Wingnuts**. Continue straight ahead here, passing more wingnuts just before a stretch of postmodern 1980s flats – embodying the transformation of London's Docklands. A path runs in front of these next to the river and joins another small open space and Elephant Lane, where you turn left by some **Field Maples**. Instead of keeping to the river on pedestrianised

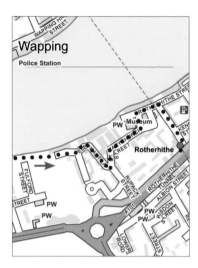

The statue of Ada Salter

Rotherhithe Street, follow Elephant Lane around to the right where, after 50 metres, you reach the Ship pub, with some **Raywood Ash** trees casting their elegant shade over its beer terrace.

Take a sharp left down St Marychurch Street, and follow it round until St Mary's Churchyard Garden, with an entrance next to the tiny coffee shop housed in the Watch House. The centrepiece of the garden is a mature **Sycamore** surrounded by a circular bench, and you'll also see, unsurprisingly, some **Trees of Heaven**.

Continue along St Marychurch Street past the charity school building dating from 1703, the former rectory and, across the road, the eighteenth-century brick-built St Mary's Church. Follow the road around the back of the church as it curves to the left, noting a **Manna Ash** tree in the grounds among the limes. Ahead of you lies the Mayflower, a delightful riverside hostelry nestled between old warehouses, with connections to the ship of that name that transported the Pilgrim Fathers to America in 1620.

Turn right on Rotherhithe Street under a **Wisteria**-clad bridge connecting two of the warehouses. On your left is the Brunel Museum, dedicated to the Victorian engineer Isambard Kingdom Brunel and his construction of the Thames Tunnel, which now takes the Overground between Rotherhithe and Wapping (the start of the Docklands walk – see page 70).

The garden is noteworthy for an elderly **False Acacia** which has, remarkably, survived some alarming arboricultural treatments, including the insertion of steel plates held in place by enormous screws, and the concreting of a split between two limbs. Attached to this is a brass plaque which, equally remarkably, is now almost covered by the growing tree. The full text reads:

Robinia pseudoacacia (False Acacia)
Introduced by Jean Robin from America in 1601 and planted widely for shipbuilding until Brunel built in iron.
This plaque and garden funded by People's Places
18th May 2005

The Mayflower at Rotherhithe

Brunel Museum False Acacia

It is wonderful to see just how much the tree has grown since 2005, and it is also worth busting the plaque's myths. The species was certainly introduced to France by Jean Robin in 1601, but may not have arrived here for a few more years, and its use in shipbuilding was minor: apparently the wood is only useful for making the pins used to fasten timbers together.

From here, turn right on Railway Avenue, past a newly planted **Monkey Puzzle** in the museum grounds, and then right again on Brunel Road to reach the entrance to Rotherhithe Station.

The Oak of Honor

A Local Community Gets Involved

Honor Oak Park to New Cross Gate

The first reason to set out on this south-east London walk is simply the views: it is undoubtedly the hilliest in the book, around the hilliest part of the capital, and you'll find exhilarating prospects of the city glittering in the distance opening up at regular intervals.

But that's not all. It takes you from some of the oldest tree cover in London – the ancient Great North Wood – to the newest, and the impressive tree planting still being done by both the local authority and its residents to green what until recently were some of London's most treeless streets.
And while there are plenty of classic, mature species to admire along the way, the real landmarks of this walk are some of the most unexpected and exotic trees you could ever hope to find in London.

Length: 5 miles (10,500 steps)
Start: Honor Oak Park Overground and National Rail station
Finish: New Cross Gate Overground and National Rail station
Shortening: Crofton Park National Rail and Brockley Overground and National Rail Stations.
Accessibility: Some steep hills, plenty of unavoidable steps, unmade paths and some busy roads
Relative Difficulty: 4/5

1 – Honor Oak to Crofton Park

Turn right out of the front of Honor Oak Park Station up Honor Oak Park, noticing the little copse of 'Kanzan' Ornamental Cherry trees on the road island opposite, and head up the hill past the allotments.

The entrance to One Tree Hill nature reserve is marked by a large oak tree on the right, a prime example of the hybrid between our two native species, Pedunculate and Sessile Oaks. If you're following this route in summer or autumn, look out for the leaves and acorns, which both have stalks, the easiest way to tell a hybrid.

At the green signs for 'Green Chain Walk' and 'One Tree Hill' turn right up the steps, and continue up through the woodland past St Augustine's Church, which has a **Cabbage Palm** by the porch, until you reach a crossroads of paths at the top. Here turn right to One Tree Hill's famous oak.

The current tree – a **Pedunculate Oak** surrounded by a circular metal fence – was planted in 1905, but legend has it that under one of its predecessors here three centuries earlier Elizabeth I picnicked on her way to Lewisham in 1602. The oak was known as the Honor Oak ever afterwards for having had the 'honor' of shading her majesty. Nearby, look out for a metal bollard embossed with 'Camberwell Parish', showing the tree's other role as a boundary marker. In Norman times a predecessor tree marked the southern boundary of the Honour of Gloucester, one of the largest baronial territories in mediaeval times.

The community round here first got involved with looking after trees back at the end of the nineteenth century, when the local golf club attempted to enclose One Tree Hill. A vociferous campaign ensued to retain it as open, common land. Not only was

View of the City from One Tree Hill

The Great North Wood

One Tree Hill, a Great North Wood remnant

It is apparent that One Tree Hill has more than one tree. Indeed, it is a woodland nature reserve, but there is one significant tree here for which the hill is named. You will have to climb steeply through the lush woodland to reach the summit in order to find the Oak of Honor, a splendid oak planted as recently as 1905, showing, surprisingly, just how fast this species can grow.

As recently as the mid-nineteenth century, a swathe of woodlands covered a great arc of south-east London from Croydon to New Cross, known as the Great North Wood. Several remnants of the wood remain, of which One Tree Hill is one. However, it is not a pristine ancient woodland, despite the presence of some old trees, and even a Wild Service Tree (an ancient woodland indicator species). It has a chequered history which is reflected in the trees – most conspicuously, the large number of London Planes.

These date back to when it was laid out as a public park, which opened at the same time as the latest iteration of the Oak of Honor was planted. It continued to be managed as a park until the 1960s. One Tree Hill shows how quickly woodland can return,

though: a restoration no doubt aided by the land's former status as woodland.

Elsewhere, places like Sydenham Hill and Dulwich Woods are further relics of the Great North Wood, while old individual trees that would once have been part of it can be glimpsed in gardens and even on streets.

Another patch of the Great North Wood you pass on this walk is the New Cross Gate Cutting. This is even less pristine than One Tree Hill, being on land created to form an embankment, originally of the Croydon Canal, but now the railway line between Brockley and New Cross Gate. So while this area was in the boundaries of the former Great North Wood, its rebound to semi-natural woodland is new and, as a result, all the more remarkable.

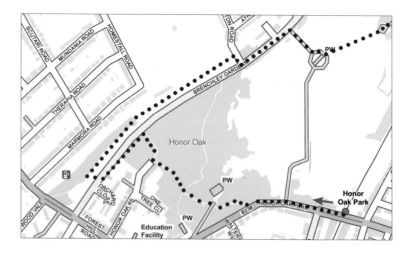

the golf club seen off: subsequently it closed altogether.

From the crossroads walk a few metres down to the clearing among the sycamores and planes, from where you get the first of today's magnificent views over London. John Betjeman, no less, described it as better than the one from Parliament Hill. There is an information board to point out the landmarks, from the London Eye in the west to the Shard and the Gherkin. The old concrete gun emplacement is a fixture from the First World War.

Now, from the crosspaths, follow the path signposted 'Ruth Sale Rise, Brenchley Gardens' down a flight of concrete steps through the wood, all the way to Brenchley Gardens at the bottom. Turn left along the pavement here, looking out for the **Wild Service Tree**, surrounded by hopeful suckers (saplings thrown up from the parent tree's roots), its leaves somewhere between a small maple and a large hawthorn, which overhangs it. When you reach a grey-brick

block of flats set back from the road, cross over Brenchley Gardens to enter the eponymous park through the gate by a Norway Maple street tree. It is something of an arboreal sweet spot.

Inside the park (also called Brenchley Gardens), you are greeted by a **Hornbeam** and a **Persian Ironwood** on the left, trees that are easy to confuse. This thoughtfully placed duo allows you to study the differ-

Persian Ironwood

ences between the two: the hornbeam is a more upright tree with toothed leaves, while the ironwood has blunter, smooth leaves and a more gangly habit.

Beyond, a fine old **Ginkgo** marks the path to the right you should follow. It passes a fine-looking **Purple Cherry Plum**, a tree much favoured in these parts, before you have a chance to examine some conifers. Compare the **Leyland Cypresses** of what might be a former hedge with some specimen **Lawson's Cypresses**, and a scrappy-looking **Juniper** (probably Meyer's). Just beyond these, hanging over the road, is the park's most prized possession, a very rare **Japanese Chestnut Oak** with glossy, sawtooth leaves. It is doing a reasonable impression of a Sweet Chestnut, but its open, regular form will give it away.

Easy to miss amid the speeding traffic, Brenchley Gardens, the course of a former

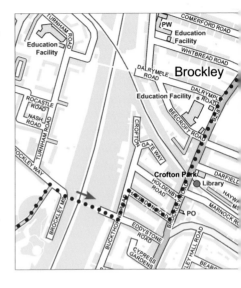

Japanese Chestnut Oak

railway line, winds along between the road and, soon, the flat, grassy expanse of Honor Oak Reservoir, over which are spread the fairways of the present-day Aquarius Golf Club. As the reservoir opens out alongside to the left, with more fabulous views of the city beyond the somewhat incongruous cupola of Honor Oak Pumping Station, the park too widens out into a grassy corridor.

Exit the park by the gate at the end, cross over Kelvington Road and continue along Brenchley Gardens the road. Just before you draw level with the entrance to Camberwell New Cemetery, look out for an aged and extremely spreading **Strawberry Tree** beyond the fence on your left. Take the zebra crossing and go into the cemetery, heading for the chapel straight ahead and passing a fine **Pin Oak** to the left. At the chapel, turn left and head towards the crematorium, looking out for a good example of a **White Poplar** among avenues of mainly hybrid poplars. You can choose to take a path to the left skirting the crematorium, or go through the gate onto the tarmac of the crematorium forecourt and driveway to admire the planting here. You will see mainly **Dawn Redwoods** and weeping **'Petiolaris' Silver Limes** (a species associated with mourning), but on the left and set back a bit a **Coastal Redwood** can be found.

Turn right out of the cemetery onto Brockley Way, and go straight on across a brown-painted metal bridge over the railway. To the left at the far side is Buckthorn Cutting nature reserve, which has occasional open days. At the crossroads turn left into Buckthorne Road – apart from

White Poplar

a solitary sapling down on the right a street completely devoid of trees. So familiar for any Londoner these days is the sight of a street – any street – lined with mature trees that when you come upon one with none, the bareness itself is almost eerily visible.

Until a few years ago this was par for the course for a great many streets in the London Borough of Lewisham – historically never one of the capital's more prosperous boroughs. But in recent years, as we shall soon see, the council has been making up for lost time, assisted by some resourceful and imaginative planting of local streets by community organisations like Street Trees for Living. In the meantime one resident on the left-hand side of Buckthorne Street has at least been doing their bit by tending a large **Cabbage Palm** in their front garden.

Turn right down Hazeldon Road and straight away you'll see evidence of Lewisham's ongoing work: a lovely tan-

American Sweetgum outside the Rivoli Ballroom

barked **Crêpe Myrtle** newly planted halfway down on the right outside a front garden luxuriantly banked with white and purple hydrangeas. (Another handy thing about street trees that have only just moved in is that they often have their nursery tag on by which to identify them.)

At the end turn left onto the main Brockley Road and follow it through the small shopping parade of Crofton Park. Outside the station is further evidence of the substantial measures being taken to beautify Lewisham's urban environment: the pavements have been widened into paved mini-piazzas, and there are new trees all the way along: no fewer than five **'Red Robin' Photinias** in wooden planters, followed by a couple of new **American Sweetgums** edged attractively with white slabs. It makes such a difference!

Brenchley Gardens

Crêpe Myrtle flowers

The Rivoli Ballroom beside these new **Sweetgums**, by the way, is a phenomenon worth visiting Crofton Park for on its own: the only 1950s-era ballroom surviving in London, despite its tatty exterior, it retains its original leather wallpaper and, with its barrel-vaulted ceiling, plush seating and chandeliers, is much in demand for video shoots as well as regular dances.

As you continue along Brockley Road look up Beecroft Road to your left: more new street-tree planting – in this case three new **'Lutescens' Whitebeam** cultivars. To your right we're now passing Brockley and Ladywell Cemetery, edged with a line of fine mature plane trees and at least one **Beech**, a species remarkably unusual in London.

Street Trees for Living

Back in 2011, the London Borough of Lewisham was a relatively unplanted place when it came to street trees. Like Hackney in the 1990s (see page 50), Lewisham Council had a host of pressing and competing demands on its finances, and planting new street trees was not considered a priority.

A new Street Trees for Living tree

Into this vacuum tentatively stepped the Brockley Society's Tree Committee.

Almost a decade later, and the humble Tree Committee has morphed into a full-blown charity, Street Trees for Living, which has made a huge difference to the urban environment throughout Lewisham. In that time, it has worked in partnership with the council to raise money for planting over 1,000 trees. Not only does it fund-raise: it has also empowered an army of volunteers to plant and maintain trees too.

Its success has been enviable: thanks to dozens of tree waterers, street reps and tree pruners, it can boast an impressive 95% survival rate for newly planted trees. This compares to a mere 80% for some boroughs who rely on contractors to do the watering and maintenance.

Not only has Street Trees for Living helped save Lewisham money and contributed to the beautification of the borough, it has also built a community of residents, businesses and the council that surely contributes to a safer, healthier and more neighbourly place in which to live, work and play.

Street Trees for Living offers an excellent model for Londoners in other parts of town who want to make a positive impact on their local environment.

2 – Hilly Fields to Brockley

At the traffic lights turn right and walk up Adelaide Road, an avenue of tall planes and Horse Chestnuts, and take a little detour around the triangle at the junction with St Margaret's Road to admire a young and rather rare **Japanese Hornbeam**. It can be differentiated from its familiar European cousin by its longer leaves and showier seed clusters. On the opposite side, look out for a recently planted **Southern Magnolia** and a **Chinese Tree Privet**.

Now we take the path up the grassy slope ahead of us past a bulbous and burry **London Plane** with great swooping limbs – it has clearly been left, unmolested by pollarders, to expand horizontally as well as vertically. This is Hilly Fields: a delightful and surprisingly expansive park that is also, clue's in the name, a not inconsiderable hill. Follow the path all the way up to the children's playground and the tennis courts, passing a low-domed **Turkey Oak**, where you can enjoy some fine views. As you look northwards, there's another stirring view above the trees to the Shard and the City's ever changing skyline, while to the south and west the upland geography of these parts is laid out, with the TV masts at Norwood and Crystal Palace punctuating the horizon.

There's a café at the top, shaded by towering plane and ash trees. Down the south side of Hilly Fields (i.e. to the right of the café, as you're looking at it) is a Stonehenge-type

The view west from Hilly Fields

Turkey Oak

installation of boulders and, beyond that, a bosky area of orchard.

To avoid retracing our steps, at all, however, and appreciate the full openness of this park, our route lies to the left of the café, down an avenue of tall planes, winding past the grassy cockpit of the cricket field on the left and the bowling green on the right. At the bottom follow the grassy edge of the park to your left along the boundary of the cricket pitch all the way to the far corner, where Hilly Fields Crescent (the road running alongside) meets Montague Avenue coming from the left.

Here, running up the edge of the park to your left, you'll find a grassy path running up through an orchard of cherry and plum trees and, sprinkled among them – a last surprise – three **Black Mulberry** trees, leaning extravagantly within their protective chicken-wire cages and, in mid-summer, generously arrayed with fruit (please leave them for all the many thousands of readers of this book to admire). Just beyond them is a further a curiosity: a **Corkscrew Willow**, a

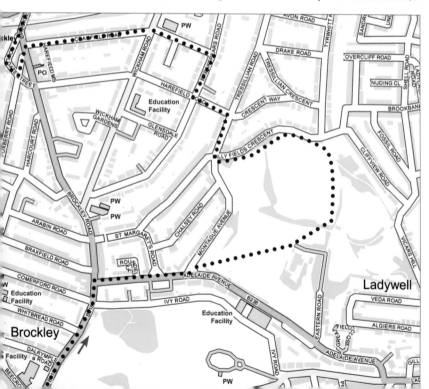

right-hand side.

Curated to favour trees indigenous to New Zealand, it features a thicket of **Lancewoods**, a strange tree that has a very different juvenile form to the mature trees now gracing this garden. It starts life as a single stem, with long, leathery leaves hanging off at 45° which must have reminded a Gothic-minded Victorian tree-namer of a medieval lance bedecked with ribbons. After about 20 years its form changes to be more conventionally tree-like (as these ones). It's thought the different forms evolved to evade browsing by extinct giant flightless moa birds that once roamed New Zealand.

But the most striking tree is not antipodean. It is a **Hybrid Strawberry Tree**, found in Greece and the eastern Mediterranean. Its amazing deep orange boughs, that exfoliate to show smooth green bark underneath, overhang the pavement. If you're passing in the autumn, you may also catch the flowers and fruit, which bloom and ripen simulta-

Monkey Puzzle

tree that looks as though it got its branches caught in an electric socket.

Back down at Hilly Fields Crescent, cross over to go north along Tressillian Road past a build-out from the pavement. A little further along, there's a recently planted **Foxglove Tree**, a wonderful addition (once it flourishes and breaks out into its unforgettable lilac-blue flowers) to any street.

Turn left down Harefield Road and then right into Breakspears Road, a street of handsome and substantial Victorian houses. Just past the left turn of Cranfield Road is an extraordinary, jungly front garden on the

Hybrid Strawberry Tree

Brockley's Persian Silk Trees

neously. The New Zealand theme continues on the street, where a rare **Long-leaved Lacebark** appears to be thriving. Could the Lancewood gardener have had anything to do with it perhaps?

Having admired two other mature garden trees: a **Copper Beech** opposite and, just a little way up, a **Monkey Puzzle**, now go down Cranfield Road. Just past the Indian Orthodox church, look out for a **Weeping Willow** up Garsington Mews, the unmetalled road next to it, and the **Hazel** overhanging the fence just before you reach the crossroads with St Peter's Church on the corner.

Cross over Wickham Road (famed as Kate Bush's address when she wrote 'Wuthering Heights' back in 1979), and continue down Cranfield Road. Two thirds of the way down this, hillier, section there's an **Elm** on the left-hand side of the street, a rare and cherishable sight, but sadly, at the time of writing, it appears to be succumbing to Dutch Elm Disease. At the bottom on the same side a new **Ginkgo** is an example of Street Trees for Living's planting activities.

At the bottom turn left along Brockley Road, cross over at the pelican crossing by the Brockley Barge pub, and go down Fox-berry Road behind the pub. You are entering Brockley's mural quarter. . . Just past it you'll see an homage to Bob Marley and, on the side wall of the house on the corner with Coulgate Road, a wonderfully surreal giant coat hanger. Now turn down Coulgate Road to Brockley Station.

Here we come upon one of the most transformative recent planting initiatives in the London Borough of Lewisham. Until a couple of years ago this was a nondescript Seventies box of a station building with a bike rack below. Now, there is a paved piazza beneath it with a new bar and pavement tables at one end, and, thanks to Street Trees for Living, no fewer than five **Persian Silk Trees** adding definition, colour and, when they're in vibrant pink bloom – a treat that can last from summer right through to early autumn – real character to the place.

Further beautification comes with the flower garden down the side of the accessible ramp to the station – planted with **Field Maples**, **Italian Cypresses** and **'Winter Orange' Small-leaved Limes** – which would grace Wisley. Where to stop for a coffee, a cool beer or an ice cream? How about, oh – Brockley Station?

Persian Silk Tree

Albizia julibrissin

Persian Silk Tree flowers and leaves

Originating from Asia, this wonderfully exotic-looking tree has been known here since 1745, and planted by gardeners ever since. But for more than two centuries, attractive but tender, feathery-leaved seedlings would feature as annuals in decorative herbaceous borders or ornamental flower beds only to be pulled up come the winter.

In recent years, a hardy strain has been introduced which has the potential to revolutionise London's tree canopy. This new Persian Silk Tree variety will happily tolerate the worst metropolitan winter (not that frosts last long in London these days), and throw out luscious, pea-green foliage the following spring. This is akin to that of Mimosa: doubly compound – that is, each leaf is branched, with each stem holding dozens of tiny leaflets – but, unlike Mimosa, and other *Acacias*, those leaves are deciduous.

But it is the flowers that are the real showstoppers, and from where the tree gets its name. Tiny handfuls of pink silk tufts can cover trees from July right through to October, followed by leguminous seed pods which stay on the leafless trees through the winter.

As the young trees at Brockley illustrate, Persian silk trees can add glamorous character to a place, and even change perceptions – in this case turning an unlikely corner into something approaching a destination. Of course, tree-planting anywhere can have a transformative effect, but perhaps a tree as striking and unusual as this one can create a sense of place with greater élan.

3 – Brockley Cross to New Cross Gate

Past the floral embankment head under the railway bridge, where another mural awaits, a retro railway-inspired sign proudly announcing 'Brockley'. It is one of many neighbourhood names that have appeared on railway bridges around south London – you may have noticed another by the Sweetgums at Crofton Park. They are the work of Lionel Stanhope who, according to *Time Out*, has 'combined his passions for street art, sign writing and south-east London'.

Cross over Brockley Cross at a zebra crossing, then over the main road by another, and head down Shardloes Road to take the first left up Millmark Grove. Follow this all the way up – its street-tree population shows a singular (maybe even slightly overpowering) proliferation of **Purple Cherry Plums**.

At the end, turn left up Vesta Road, past Brockley Nature Reserve (aka New Cross Gate Cutting), a London Wildlife Trust reserve on the right. It is rarely open, but is

New Cross Gate Cutting

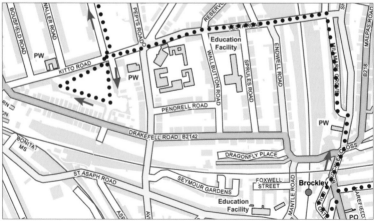

View west from Telegraph Hill

a remarkable place: a secondary woodland on a railway embankment that was, until less than a century ago, allotments. The London Wildlife Trust, which has managed it for the last 30 years, has transformed it into a sylvan idyll where rare orchids in the shape of **Broad-leaved Helleborine** now grow in its shade.

At the end of Vesta Road you reach Telegraph Hill: the last of the south-east London summits we surmount today – though not quite the last great view. It is so named because in the eighteenth century the East India Company established a telegraph station here (there was another atop One Tree Hill), to relay news of its ships, presumably en route to the London docks, being sighted in the Channel.

Telegraph Hill has not one but two delectable parks, and we'll visit the upper one (on the left) first, which is next door to the Hill Station, a recommended refreshment stop. This upper park – with its tennis courts the more 'active' of the two – is worth a look

Service Tree of Fountainebleau

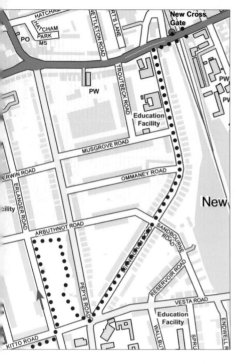

horticultural pantheon.

Now go back across the road to the corner of Erlanger Road, like the streets on the other side of the park a steeply descending avenue of mature planes. **London Planes** are steady growers, and these are regularly and rigorously pollarded to ensure they never exceed a certain height, so the council can be sure that any subsidence claims for local properties are not down to oversized street trees sucking up more than their fair share of moisture.

Enter the Lower Park at the south-west, Kitto Road entrance and follow the winding path all the way down. This park has in recent years been extensively renovated and re-landscaped, and is now such a pleasantly picturesque spot that we're going to perambulate it by doubling back up the eastern side, around the skatepark, to exit by the gate in the top-left corner.

The first tree that strikes you is a huge old leaning Ash with a strange growth

for its view: more open than either One Tree Hill or Hilly Fields, it offers a fine prospect of west London, and is a grand place for a picnic. Having said that, there are some quietly interesting trees here too – look out for a very fine **Field Maple** and, dotted around the perimeter, two or three **Service Trees of Fontainebleau**.

This extravagantly-named species in the *Sorbus* genus has leaves close to a Whitebeam, but rather spikier. There are dozens of very specific *Sorbus* species found all over Europe and Asia, often with very local distributions. Most remain in obscurity, found only in inaccessible gorges or remote mountainsides, but this Parisian tree somehow bucked the trend and entered the

'Pendula' Wych Elm

Plane pollards on Jerningham Road

around its lower trunk. This is a graft mark, showing where the upper tree was attached to rootstock in order to clonally reproduce a cultivar with specific characteristics. In this case it appears to be a rare **'Pendula'** cultivar of **Narrow-leaved Ash**. About a third of the way down, the small lake on the left has been consecrated as a memorial to the end of the slave trade. Continuing down past the larger lake on the right, there's a pair of **Weeping Willows**. One is the common **'Golden'** cultivar, while the other, larger and greyer, looks like **'Salamon's'**.

As you reach the bottom of the park, turn right and walk past a fine **Honey Locust** before making your way back uphill to the south-east exit. On your way, you will notice a **'Pendula' Wych Elm** on your right, a rather lovely old-fashioned tree typical of municipal parks. Finally, as you leave the park, look out for the huge **Turkey Oak** in the corner along

Honey Locust

Wellingtonia or Giant Redwood?

The New Cross Gate Giant Redwood

Giving trees names can be a fraught business, and even when they have been named, science can often throw a spanner in the works as botanical knowledge evolves.

Of course, trees, and indeed any living thing, usually have two or more names. The most important is the scientific or Latin name, an internationally accepted term that places a species within taxonomic hierarchies, and is handy when discussing a species across cultural boundaries. Some living things, usually very small ones, can be known just by their scientific name, as no one has bothered to give it a common one. But trees, by and large, do have common names – names that have evolved over the years – and sometimes lots of them.

The Giant Redwood is a case in point. In the UK, it is often known as 'Wellingtonia', a scientific-sounding name that remembers the Duke of Wellington (he of boot fame), who died in 1852. In fact, the scientific name *Wellingtonia gigantea* was suggested for

these remarkable big trees in 1853, soon after their 'discovery', by the English botanist John Lindley. Unfortunately, there was already a genus of unrelated plants named *Wellingtonia*, and it wasn't until 1939 that the scientific name *Sequoiadendron giganteum* was fixed. But in the UK, that Wellingtonia epithet persisted, having been popularised by a national desire to memorialise the boot Duke.

The Americans, understandably, were not so keen on a tree indigenous to California being named after a British soldier and politician. The accepted scientific name therefore resonates with colonial and scientific nuances, and draws attention to both a botanical feature – the ordering of seeds in cones – and remembers a Native American polymath: Sequoyah.

Approaching New Cross

with some fine **'Fastigiata' Hornbeams**. Now head down Jerningham Road all the way to the bottom, pausing at Arbuthnot Road on your left to see another example of Street Trees for Living's new planting: this time a **Chinese Scarlet Rowan**. About halfway down is is a good spot to admire a final view of the shining Shard and its skyscraping neighbours over Jerningham Road's well-pollarded planes.

In just the length of this street you'll have descended from the tranquility of Telegraph Hill to the roaring traffic of the A2; from the former landscape of the Great North Wood, to the Thames floodplain below. A front garden **'Silver Queen' Kohuhu** from New Zealand signals the approach of New Cross Road. Cross over to New Cross Gate Station. But this tree walk is not quite done. There is one last, glorious surprise.

Just to the right of the station entrance, past a few shops, peer over the bridge above the railway and . . . good grief! All on its own beside the tracks, on the edge of a patch of waste ground: a lone sentinel: conical in shape, with an eponymously red-barked trunk: *Sequoiadendron giganteum*: a native of the Sierra Nevada in California, where it grows on western mountain slopes. A **Giant Redwood**. At New Cross Gate. Who planted it here is a mystery. It certainly wouldn't appear to have seeded itself, but there it is, surely a Great Tree of London.

We started out, on One Tree Hill, at the scene of a celebrated – and thankfully successful – attempt to save a patch of common land and the site of generations of English oaks, a species that could not be more representatively traditional, and we finish at another monumental specimen that could not be more exotic in these parts. If you're taking a southbound train home from Platform 4 you'll get an even closer, more dwarfing view.

Chinese Tree Privet in Churchill Gardens

Architectural Utopias Among the Trees

A Pimlico Circular

Waves of large-scale utopian developments have left
their mark on Pimlico and Westminster over the past 200
years. From Pimlico's stuccoed terraces and Westminster's
fin-de-siècle Millbank Estate to the modernist Churchill
Gardens estate, trees have always been part of the plan to
humanise these grand architectural visions.
In early nineteenth century Pimlico, trees were confined
to garden squares, but by the time the Millbank Estate was
completed at the end of the century, no urban plan would
be complete without a complement of London Planes.
Fifty years later, Churchill Gardens provided state-of-the-art
modern living among an arboretum, while in recent years
Westminster Council has been planting up formerly treeless
streets wherever it can with all manner of interesting trees,
although one species does tend to be favoured ...

Length: 2.5 miles (5,000 steps)
Start and Finish: Pimlico Tube station (Victoria Line)
Accessibility: Pavements and level surfaces, crossing some busy roads
Relative Difficulty: 2/5

1 – Bessborough Street to Churchill Gardens

Leaving Pimlico Tube station by the Bessborough Street entrance, head west past the spire of St Saviour's church and then left into St George's Square with Pimlico Academy on your right.

The square proper, actually a long rectangle, starts just after the church. It is a formal garden square, typical of many encountered in London, but, unlike many in these rarefied postcodes, St George's is open to the public. There's little to see inside it, however, and its chief attractions are visible from the pavement.

perhaps, and might continue skywards for at least another 180 years.

The Pimlico Academy facing the north-west corner of the square occupies land once covered with grand early-Victorian terraces similar to those lining its south-western and eastern sides. These were pulled down during post-war slum clearances,

Pimlico School in the 1970s

These are the towering **London Planes**, interspersed with a few **Sycamores** that line the perimeter. Since the square and its five-storey, stuccoed terraces were constructed between 1839 and 1843, that makes the planes about 180 years old. This is relatively old for London's planes – most of its large, city-defining trees were planted between 1870 and 1914. These are impressive, just entering their early maturity,

and supplanted in the late 1960s by the original Pimlico School. A Brutalist concrete landmark once described – positively – as a battleship, it epitomised a modern vision of the inspirational and transformative nature of education. Sadly, this iconic building suffered from years of neglect and, despite calls for it to be protected by architectural luminaries, was itself demolished in 2010.

Beyond the school, turn right into

Chichester Street, with the massed bulk of Dolphin Square on your left. This imposing, vaguely Art Deco affair of brick and stone squats somewhat ostentatiously on an area large enough to contain 1,250 flats. Since their construction, they have been much favoured as pied-à-terres by generations of politicians, mandarins and even royalty. They entirely surround and effectively enclose what is said to be a bucolic landscaped garden, which you may be able to glimpse through the gates either side of the main entrance. Instead of this private Eden, we shall examine the trees lining Chichester Street.

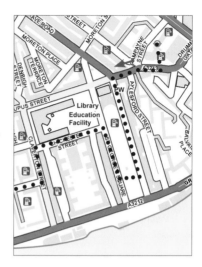

The larger, well-spaced trees are **Small-leaved Limes**, a native species now rare in semi-natural habitats, but well-suited for the pavement. In the past, hybrid Common Limes were the species of choice for urban planting, but their symbiotic relationship with the honeydew-excreting aphids that are the bane of car owners has ensured they are now less favoured. On the Dolphin Square side, the trees are pears: neat **Chanticleer Pears**, and more traditional **'Beech Hill' Pears**, a cultivar of the domestic pear.

'Beech Hill' Pear by Dolphin Square

At the end of Chichester Street we turn left into Claverton Street, still complete with a grand stuccoed terrace on its eastern side. But on its west side a functional low-rise slab block has replaced the Victoriana. The trees on this street represent different planting periods in line with the architecture. Those on the east are young, maybe 20 years old, whereas the western trees are older, probably planted when the flats were completed during the 1970s. The species represent their times of planting and the preferences of planners over the years as well. The eastern trees are more **Chanticleer Pears**.

The older western trees are another hardy staple, **Italian Alders**, favoured by an earlier generation of urban planters. They are not infrequent, particularly in central London where their ability to thrive in poor, rubble-rich soil appears to have endeared them to councils in the late twentieth century.

Pimlico

Pimlico is, in central London terms, a relatively little-visited corner. Lying south and east of Victoria Station and the railway lines that feed into it, and west of Vauxhall Bridge Road, it was originally conceived as a southern extension of always well-to-do Belgravia to the north.

'Raywood' Ash tree against Pimlico stucco

It was laid out on an area of fields and marshes in the 1820s by Thomas Cubitt, the builder of Belgravia and Bloomsbury. Cubitt's vision, still largely intact, was for a mesh of stucco-terrace-lined streets interspersed with garden squares such as St George's, Warwick and Eccelstone.

In the first half or the nineteenth century, trees and green spaces were seen as integral to the development of new, planned districts like Pimlico. However their place in these grand schemes was deemed to be the squares. Tree-lined avenues and residential streets were not yet in vogue, London's planned public parks were several decades away, and townhouses usually faced directly onto roads with no front gardens.

Squares, then, were the focus for taking the air and promenading under shady canopies generally provided by London Planes, a species frequent in squares from Berkeley and Bedford to Bloomsbury and Russell. Of Pimlico's squares, St George's has best retained its original character. Many others have, in later decades, been transformed into secluded gardens. Eccelstone is a prime example.

By the end of the nineteenth century, Pimlico had started to decline, and at the turn of the twentieth century, areas towards the south and east had become slums. Dolphin Square partly revived its fortunes in the 1930s, but following the Second World War significant swathes were demolished to make way for the Churchill Gardens, Lillington and Longmoore Gardens estates, as well as for Pimlico School.

Around the turn of the millennium, the once treeless streets of nineteenth-century Pimlico have undergone another, quieter transformation. Trees have been planted along most; some, like the east side of Claverton Street, have been planted directly into the pavement. In Sussex Street, space for trees has been reclaimed from the road, while the intersection of Denbigh and Charlwood Streets has been blocked by a tree-shaded mini-piazza.

2 – Churchill Gardens to Vauxhall Bridge Road

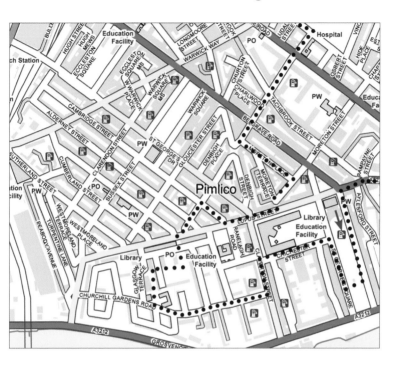

A gap in the wall of modernist flats takes us onto Churchill Gardens Road and into the 32 acres of the Churchill Gardens estate. Continue along this road past a purple-leaved **'Crimson King' Norway Maple**, a species that, in its various forms, has been planted all over London to the point that it is the second most frequent city tree after the **London Plane**. It looks similar to the familiar sycamore, but can be differentiated by its spikier leaves and more fissured bark. The myriad forms available, however, mean it may be unfamiliar to many.

Head under Moyle House and enter the older core of the estate, where yellow-brick slab blocks flank the road. The first of these

on the left is Keats House, whose gardens are worth a sidestep to see. The large trees on the left consist of a **Red Oak** and, just beyond it, a **Tree of Heaven**, a handsome, though short-lived, species originating

'Crimson King' Norway Maple

'Fastigiata' Hornbeam

from Asia (see page 104), now considered to be something of a pest. When the time comes, this mature example is unlikely to be replaced with another.

After Tyrell House, there's a fine **Ash** and a lovely **'Fastigiata' Hornbeam**, a cultivar with a particularly neat, conical appearance, known as 'Fastigiata' in reference to the habit of producing upward-sweeping branches, a characteristic which becomes less pronounced with age. On your way back up to Churchill Gardens Road, look out for a couple of very pretty **Cootamundra Wattles**, with greyish-mauve leaves and sparse yellow flowers in winter, and a **Dessert Pear**, all on your right.

Continue through the estate noting, just after Coleridge House on the right, a large purple-leaved **'Spaethii' Sycamore** and a younger **Southern Catalpa** in the landscaped gardens. A detour here will also reveal a **Scarlet Thorn**, a North American hawthorn with larger leaves than our native species, and, by the bin store (a listed feature), a rare **Varnish Tree**. Be careful with this tree – it's poisonous. It is native to east Asia, and in Japan it is valued for the lacquer produced from its toxic sap.

Varnish Tree

Back on Churchill Gardens Road, the side wall of Shelley House on the left proudly sports a blue plaque awarded in 1951 when the first five blocks of the new estate received the Festival of Britain Merit Award.

Just beyond Shelley House lies Churchill Gardens' tallest feature, the Accumulator Tower, a frosted-glass-clad structure once used to provide communal heating for the estate. Beyond the Accumulator Tower, Maitland House hosts a pair of luxuriant glossy-leaved **White Mulberries**, but a tree at the end of the walkway next to Bramwell House may have caught your eye. It is a huge **Nettle Tree**, surely one of London's largest.

Follow the road as it curves round through the buildings, gardens and trees, particularly noting a large evergreen **Chinese Tree Privet** and a **Japanese Pagoda Tree** between Ripley and Wilkins Houses on the left. Just before Chippendale House, turn right, noting a mature **Golden Rain Tree** on your left and the large, domed **Hornbeam** overhanging the street just beyond, another of many excellent examples of the 'Fastigiata' cultivar on the estate.

Beyond Wedgwood House, and before a fine group of trees including yet another **'Fastigiata' Hornbeam** and a **Chinese Tree Privet**, tucked away in the Churchill Gardens Wildflower Garden, take the path off to the right. This passes the northern end of Lutyens House and emerges on the street. Follow it ahead briefly, and take a path off to the right past the Churchill Gardens Residents' Hall, where, in the garden to your right, a young **Handkerchief Tree** has been planted. Follow the main path under Blackstone House to arrive at the estate's central piazza, a fine example of a mid-century civic open space.

Cross the piazza – Johnson's Place –

Johnson's Place

Japanese Pagoda Trees frame Churchill Gardens

under the shade of **Small-leaved Limes** and **Italian Alders**. Turn left past Langdale House and leave the sanctuary of Churchill Gardens between Littleton and De Quincey Houses, to emerge on Lupus Street.

Take the pelican crossing over Lupus Street and turn right in the direction of St Saviour's church spire in the distance. After a few metres turn left on Charlwood Street, following it over Alderney Street where, on your left, you pass a pair of **'Excelsum superbum'** variegated **Chinese Tree Privets**.

Outside Russell House, a pair of **Japanese Pagoda Trees** are thriving, while just round the corner, on Cambridge Street, a pair of very unusual **Chestnut-leaved Oaks** can be seen. These rare trees from Iran appear to do better in London's climate than in their Caucasian Mountain homeland: a tree planted at Kew in 1843 is the largest

tree in its collection.

From here, turn back down Cambridge Street to rejoin Lupus Street, where you turn left. After another 70 metres, at the junction with St George's Road, take a little detour to examine the planting on the corner with Denbigh Street, where a 1995 statue of Thomas Cubitt, the builder of Pimlico, is surrounded by a selection of trees. There's a pair of **London Planes** outside the Dolphin pub, but across the road shading the statue is a fine **Indian Horse Chestnut**.

Similar to the European common horse chestnut, this species flowers later, is perhaps a more elegant tree and, crucially, is not subject to leaf-miner attack, which disfigures the leaves of the familiar conker tree by high summer. It also produces a crop of chestnuts in the autumn: slightly smaller, rounder and darker than those of the European tree, they are potentially harder, so tactical advantages could be gained by keen conker players.

Continue west along Lupus Street until the next turning into Moreton Terrace, blocked to traffic by an evergreen **Mimosa**. It is doing very well in this frontline spot, soaking up reflected heat from the buildings and hard surfaces surrounding it. It is only around 20 years old, but already it has grown to fill this space and become a local landmark, noted for its copious, gorgeously scented yellow flowers that explode somewhat unexpectedly in February.

Mimosa, or silver wattle, originates from Australia, and as we fork right off Moreton Terrace into Moreton Street more antipodean plants appear. Small and rather ungainly but, caught at the right time of year, laden with striking red flower spikes, these are **Bottlebrush Trees**. Take the next left onto Moreton Place, where a potential clue to the inspiration behind this exotic planting scheme can be found. Number 7 boasts a blue plaque remembering Billy Hughes, the former Australian Prime Minister, who was born here in 1862.

As Moreton Place ends at Charlwood Street, turn right, but note behind you the remodelled crossroads now blocked by a paved area planted with **Ginkgos**. Apart from these fascinating ancient trees, a species that evolved even before the dinosaurs, the streets leading off are almost exclusively planted with **Chanticleer Pears**.

The trees in these parts are young, and represent Westminster's pioneering (and no doubt expensive) evolution of Pimlico's streetscapes. What were, for a century and

a half, treeless thoroughfares are in the process of being transformed into softer, greener streets. Despite trees not having been part of Cubitt's original design for the Pimlico, their presence serves only to enhance the elegant architecture.

Continue west, crossing Belgrave Road and Tachbrook Street, and pass through the Lillington Gardens estate, a series of brick ziggurats completed in 1971 and representing the last major redevelopment of Pimlico. You'll see a **Cypress Oak** on your right and a **European Alder** on your left here. Beyond, we cross Vauxhall Bridge Road and enter Westminster.

'Chanticleer' Pears

Churchill Gardens

London's Second World War destruction provided planners with a rare opportunity to re-build a modern city. Sir Patrick Abercrombie's Greater London Plan of 1944 identified how war-damaged and slum housing could be cleared to make way for spacious modern homes with proper sanitation along with public open spaces. Born out of this optimistic vision, the Churchill Gardens estate was planned to provide 1,600 new homes.

Churchill Gardens in the 1960s

As well as one of the first, Churchill Gardens is one of the largest and most ambitious social housing developments in the UK. Several innovations are at its heart, notably the Accumulator Tower, a structure designed to hold hot water for heating the entire estate, which was pumped directly from Battersea Power Station across the river.

Perhaps the most striking thing about the estate is how it is enveloped by green space and mature trees. Unlike the eighteenth- and nineteenth-century urban ideal emphasising the separation of houses and greenery, Churchill Gardens represents a modern vision of living among the trees. At every turn, mature hornbeams, tree privets, southern catalpas and other species are present. Well-kept gardens, tended by residents, pop up all over, and secret green corners among the tower blocks offer natural sanctuaries.

There is a suggestion – repeated by the residents' association – that the estate's original tree planting was carried out in collaboration with Kew Gardens. Whether this is accurate or not is perhaps a detail: the fact is, Churchill Gardens is full of fine, well-tended trees that the people who live here are proud of and that help to foster a palpable sense of place and community.

Designed by the young architectural practice Powell and Moya, the estate's development started in 1946, with the final blocks – those on the western side of Claverton Street – not completed until the 1970s. It is now a conservation area, with several of the oldest blocks listed by English Heritage. Walking through the estate, it is possible to experience the utopian vision of large-scale planned housing.

3 – Vincent Square to the Millbank Estate

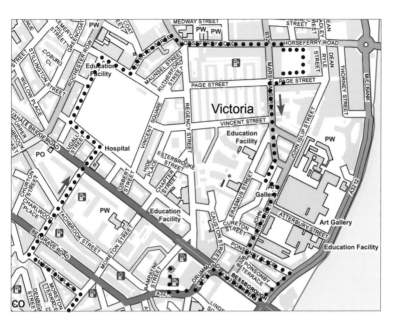

From the east side of Vauxhall Bridge Road, continue west down Bloomburg Street for a short distance to arrive at Vincent Square.

Another square with a perimeter of **London Planes**, Vincent Square is large, with its interior given over to Westminster School's playing fields. The trees here are suitably grand and old, although maybe not quite as old as those in St George's Square. In their distant past, these trees may have been managed more severely than they are today; nowadays they have been largely left to their own devices, and tower above the surrounding streets. But look carefully and you might discern how at one time they were pollarded a few metres above ground, resulting in the development of multiple leading branches.

From Bloomburg Street, turn left and head round the square in a clockwise direction, passing the RHS Lindley Library on the west side, before turning off onto Elverton Street past a row of **'Amber Beauty' Manchurian Cherries**. At the next left turn, Greycoat Street, it is worth stopping to admire a **Ginkgo** outside the former RHS exhibition halls. It is a particularly fine example, and relatively mature compared to most of those found on London's streets.

But what is most interesting is that this is a female. Ginkgos are dioecious, meaning each individual is one gender. London's trees tend to be monoecious, meaning individual plants have both male and female flowering parts, leading to most trees bearing fruit or seeds. The vast majority of Ginkgos

Female Ginkgo on Greycoat Street

Himalayan birches by reddish, flaking bark in upper branches. Turn right into Horseferry Road, which you follow as it curves round past the junction with Regency Street for another 150 metres before turning into the oasis of St John's Gardens. A former churchyard connected to St John's Smith Square, it became a park in the 1880s and has retained its Victorian character ever since. Dominated by massive London Planes, it has some other trees to admire too.

By the south-eastern gate, a non-cultivar **Hornbeam** acts as a point of reference to compare with those fastigiate trees seen in the Churchill Gardens Estate. Next to it is a very rare **'Lorbergii' Norway Maple**, with deeply cut leaves that make it very difficult to identify. Towards the south-west is a striking Japanese **Katsura** with delicate heart-shaped leaves, while across towards the north-west corner is perhaps the Gardens' most memorable tree: an enormous **Ginkgo**. It is certainly the largest and possibly the

are male: a gender preferred by planters because they don't bear fruit. Ginkgo fruits (strictly speaking, seeds surrounded by a fleshy, fruit-like outer skin) contain a chemical producing an extremely unpleasant odour which becomes all too apparent in the autumn as they fall to the ground. While many find this smell – likened to vomit – unpleasant, the male flowers can also cause irritation for those who suffer from hay fever.

Continue down Elverton Street, recently planted with **Juneberries** and white-trunked **Chinese Red Birches**, a species distinguishable from glistening-trunked

Katsura leaves

oldest example encountered on any of the walks in this book.

Take the exit near to the Ginkgo and turn right on Page Street, before turning left on Marsham Street, which is punctuated only by a pair of fine **Italian Alders** outside the Art Deco block, Westminster Gardens. Marsham Street eventually leads to a cross-roads with multiple roads leading through the pitched-roofed, redbrick blocks of the Millbank Estate.

Thirty-two blocks are positioned at jaunty angles, separated by **London Plane**-lined streets. The trees were planted at the same time the estate was constructed at the turn of the twentieth century, and so they are now well over a century old. They have been well managed over the years, with their branches regularly pollarded to keep them trim.

Indeed, they are at their finest in winter, when their regular, skeletal forms are best appreciated against the attractive Arts and Crafts architecture. In the dozen decades since their planting, the trees have started to lean away from the buildings in order to maximise their leaves' exposure to sunlight, producing a splendid urban hollow-way effect, accentuated in the winter.

Follow Herrick Street as it loops past Millbank Gardens on the left, where some of the planes have been replaced by **Chanticleer Pears** – a great shame, especially in such an architecturally and arboreally coherent scheme. Halfway along Milbank Gardens, pause to look right up St Oswulf Street at one of the estate's best views: a short but complete avenue of **London Planes** framing the handsome facade of

Chanticleer Pear

Pyrus calleryana 'Chanticleer'

Chanticleer pear trees, are – surprisingly, perhaps – one of the most frequently planted tree species in London.

They are cultivars (named forms akin to rose or apple varieties) of the Asian callery pear. You might be hard pressed to recognise the Chanticleer as a pear tree, though: it flowers fleetingly in March and by autumn has produced only inconsequential fruits.

Chanticleers are much admired by many urban tree planters, however. They have many features that recommend them for city life: they are tough, easy to establish and relatively small. They require little maintenance, and they will keep their neat shape without lots of expensive pruning. They burst into flower quite early in the year, though not a patch on glamorous ornamental cherries, and in the late autumn their leaves turn an attractive golden colour.

But for all their pluses, they may not be such a wonder tree. They are insignificant, easily missed and rather anonymous. So perhaps they will be a tree associated with a particular era – the early twenty-first century – and as the horticulture industry introduces better, more attractive trees, they will fall out of favour.

Cypress Oak outside the Morpeth Arms

Hogarth House. Turn left here into the gardens, among the **Chusan** and **Cabbage Palms**, looking out for another **Katsura** tree on the left. These striking Japanese trees have delicate, heart-shaped, or cordate, leaves that turn attractive colours in the autumn. There is also a conundrum present here in the shape of several rare white-beams: these have pointed, cherry-type leaves, which points to them possibly being **Himalayan Whitebeams**, but a firm ID has eluded this author.

Emerge from Millbank Gardens onto John Islip Street, a particularly well-kept plane-lined avenue, and turn right past Tate Britain. Several more blocks of the Millbank Estate are on our right, before a dry concrete moat forms the boundary of the estate. This feature predates the estate, as it was once the boundary ditch of the Millbank Prison. Turn left off John Islip Street onto treeless Ponsonby Place, a street once loomed over by the prison, and turn right at the end past a **Cypress Oak** and the Mor-peth Arms onto Millbank. The Morpeth Arms was opened in 1845 to provide refreshment for prison warders, and more recently has been a popular haunt for Tate visitors. The building must have adapted part of the old prison, as the basement (or dungeon) still contains a number of dank cells.

Turn right onto Millbank, and right again onto Vauxhall Bridge Road, heading up past the Lithuanian Embassy and crossing by the White Swan. Continue along Drum-mond Gate, which curves round to the right where it becomes Bessborough Street, where, just beyond a solitary **London Plane**, the subway slopes into Pimlico Station.

Millbank Estate

St Oswulf Street

The ambitious Arts and Crafts-influenced Millbank Estate was constructed between 1899 and 1902 by the recently formed London County Council (LCC). This was its second social housing development, the first being the smaller Boundary Estate in Shoreditch.

The estate's 17 housing blocks were built to house people displaced from slum clearances, and the 562 new flats they contained were a great improvement on the insanitary conditions in which many working people had been forced to live. The sense of improvement, both in the high- quality architecture and access to modern conveniences, continued in the names given to the buildings: each is named after a British artist whose work was admired at the time (although these days some may not spring immediately to mind).

The blocks were constructed from recycled red bricks taken from the vast Millbank Prison that once covered the land where the estate and Tate Britain now stand. Prisoners from all over Great Britain sentenced to deportation were held here before being shipped to penal colonies in far-flung corners of the empire.

Integral to the design of the estate was the inclusion of open space and the provision of trees. While not on the scale of Churchill Gardens, these were radical developments at the time. The communal, mostly paved, outdoor space is tucked away between the blocks, and the trees planted over 120 years ago still grace the streets running between them.

When the estate was built, London was in the midst of its plane tree craze and, unsurprisingly, the trees planted here are London Planes. They appeared to be the perfect tree for cities: attractive, fast-growing and able to cope with the industrial pollution of the time. Over the years, the trees have been well cared for, having been regularly pollarded to keep them an appropriate size and shape for their location.

Marc Bolan shrine.

Rock Family Trees

Barnes to Battersea Power Station

This walk is inspired by the publisher of this book's musical passion, and begins at the only tree in this guide to have become a genuine, historic monument – and of a rather unexpected kind. It kicks off an exploration of south-west London's musical heritage, and in particular the classic era of rock music from the early sixties to the mid-eighties, the heyday of acts like the Rolling Stones and Pink Floyd. It's a journey through a cultural epoch, too: the Swinging Sixties, and especially the fashions it spawned.

But it's also a walk of consistent arboreal interest, and for London a remarkably sylvan one, leading through woods and across commons and greens, taking in a magnificent nineteenth-century cemetery and finishing in one of London's first and largest parks. It's quite a long walk – a whole day, perhaps, to do it justice – but it can be broken or shortened at one of several railway or Tube stations along the way.

Length: 7 miles (15,000 steps)
Start: Barnes National Rail station
Finish: Battersea Park National Rail, or Battersea Power Station (Northern Line – scheduled to open late 2021)
Shortening: Putney Bridge or Fulham Broadway Tube stations (District Line)
Accessibility: Pavements and level surfaces, crossing some busy roads and a park
Relative Difficulty: 3/5

1 – Barnes to Putney Bridge

Leave Barnes Station on the London platform side, go through the tunnel next to the entrance to Platform 1 and follow the tarmac path alongside the railway line, with Barnes Common on your left visible behind the screen of **Ashes, Limes, Oaks** and **Sycamores.**

Go up a wooden staircase on your right to the road bridge over the railway and cross the road – Queen's Ride – to Gipsy Lane opposite. A few metres down on the right, through a gap in the trees, descend the wooden steps to a bosky, scrub-fringed road, and shortly on your right you'll come upon the shrine to Marc Bolan.

From the late sixties to the early seventies Marc Bolan, the elfin leader of the glam rock band T. Rex, was briefly one of the biggest names in the music world – indeed, along with David Bowie, one of the first to quite deliberately aim at and achieve rock stardom – with hits like 'Ride a White Swan',

'Hot Love' and 'Get It On'. In those days rock stars usually met an untimely death through a heroic consumption of drink and drugs, but on 16 September 1977 Bolan's Mini left the road above and, legend has it, collided with a **Sycamore** tree, and he was dead just before his thirtieth birthday.

Even in 2020 this shrine is impressively curated: a plaque, a bust of Bolan, a noticeboard papered with tributes, and bunches of flowers recently left. As for the guilty sycamore, the specimen currently festooned with 7-inch singles and a picture of two white swans is a pretty unimpressive thing – spindly, multi-trunked, more of an overgrown sapling – that hardly looks capable of mortal injury.

But perhaps it never was? The black and white news photos of the crash site appear to show a scarred trunk situated where, bizarrely, an ornamental barrel stands today. There is some speculation that it was actually a metal fence – since replaced by crash barriers – that did the damage, and the tree actually prevented the car from tumbling down the embankment (perhaps saving his girlfriend Gloria Jones's life).

Retrace your steps to the wooden staircase on the road bridge, and at the bottom turn right along the path. Cross over Common Road and follow the muddy path opposite through Barnes Common nature reserve. At a crossroads of paths by a tall,

Blasted Deodar Cedar

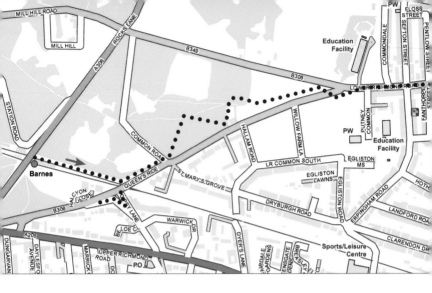

spreading **Pedunculate Oak** turn right, and when you reach a wall, another elderly oak and a sign for 'Putney Lower Common' go straight ahead to follow a track across open grassland, keeping close to the road and passing a gaunt **Deodar Cedar** on the right.

Emerging on the road again opposite All Saints, Putney church, turn left to the junction and bear right onto the Lower Richmond Road, which you now follow for 900 metres all the way to Putney Bridge. The first stretch is lined with mature **Common Limes**, **Horse Chestnuts**, **Sycamores** and **London Planes**, but soon these peter out and for most of its length this is a rather barren thoroughfare.

But there are some highlights: look out for a yellow-flowering Californian Flannelbush in a front garden just down Stanbridge Road on your right. Just past Festing Road, a row of front gardens sport a **Honey Locust**, a splendid **Southern Magnolia**, a mature **Silver Birch** and an exotic-looking **Cabbage Palm**.

Across the road on your right you come to the Half Moon Hotel, the first of several historic pub music venues on this tree tour, and sadly the only one still committed to regular live music. London's pub music circuit came into its own in the first half of the seventies in reaction against the tendency for prog rock acts like Pink Floyd and Yes

Chonosuki Crabapple outside the Half Moon

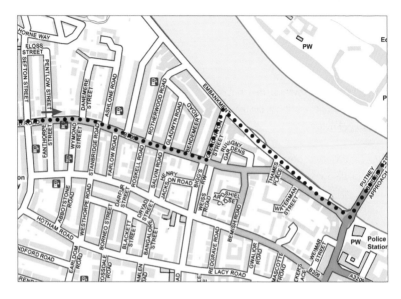

to confine their live appearances to vast, pyrotechnical pageants in enormodomes. In recent years the Half Moon's fare has tended towards tribute bands, but in its day it was one of so many pub-rock venues that bands could literally tour London boozers full-time. These venues helped to launch the careers of such gritty musicians as the great Ian Dury, Canvey Island's finest, Dr Feelgood, and Graham Parker and the Rumour. The young and bedraggled **Chonosuki Crabapple** on the other side of the road, one of very few street trees on this stretch, is hardly a fitting monument.

A few doors down you'll come upon the London Mini Centre, where you can get a very good idea of just how minute Minis like Bolan's were. You could actually fit a vintage one inside a modern Mini Cooper.

Take a left on Glendarvon Street, lined with an attractive array of **Rowans**, some unidentified ornamental cherries and a

Swedish Whitebeam or two, and follow it down to the Thames. This is Putney Embankment, with rowing-club boathouses to your left, and a procession of tall, mature planes, leaning towards the river for the light, leading the way to Putney Bridge. Just before the bridge, notice a pair of tall slim **'Fastigiata' Golden Rain Trees** on the eastern side of Thames Place opposite the Duke's Head, examples of this very unusual columnar cultivar.

Swedish Whitebeam

Sycamore

Acer pseudoplatanus

Sycamores are controversial trees. Not only have they been implicated in the death of a much-admired glam rock star, but they are also accused of muscling in on quieter, undemonstrative 'native' trees.

European sycamores are a type of maple that naturally occurs on the near-continent, but their pollen doesn't appear in the British fossil record even after the last ice age. It's not known exactly when they arrived here or how, but for some the fact they weren't here 10,000 years ago means they should be classed as non-native and therefore suspicious.

By the eighteenth century, however, they had become a popular tree for ornamental planting, although in the seventeenth century the diarist and dendrophile John Evelyn was not so keen:

for the honey-dew leaves, which fall early (like those of the ash) turn to mucilage and noxious insects, and putrefy with the first moisture of the season, so as they contaminate and mar our walks; and are therefore, by my consent, to be banished from all curious gardens and avenues.

Now, though, love them or loathe them, Sycamores are here to stay. They reproduce easily and abundantly, and provide homes for many other creatures. Their distinctive leaves adorn railway embankments, hedges, cemeteries and woodlands throughout London; they are not subject to significant pests and diseases (at least for now), and a mature Sycamore can be a very handsome sight.

Perhaps it is time we embrace this fine tree unreservedly, and accept it as just another Londoner.

2 – Fulham to Brompton Cemetery

Bishop's Park from Putney Bridge

Cross Putney Bridge on its eastern (right-hand) side. At the far end there is Bishop's Park on the left, with a **Nootka** and a **Lawson's Cypress**, and, visible along the river bank, a fine row of **London Planes**. These giants have benefitted from their position next to the river – with their feet in the water – and since being planted in 1893 have become as large as trees a century older in other parts of London.

Follow Fulham High Street straight on to the traffic lights past All Saints, Fulham, surrounded by a fine collection of **London Planes** and at least one Tree of Heaven. We turn right into New King's Road, but iIf you were to continue straight on and branch off up Fulham Palace Road you'd come to what used to be yet another famous rock pub, the Greyhound, where most of the top acts from the 1970s onwards, cut their teeth. The Jam supporting Thin Lizzy there must have been

a good one. 'Used to be' is now the common fate of most of these venues, though: a consequence of rising rents, tougher noise restrictions, a changing music scene and the gastro-fication of pubs in now-sedate residential parts.

When New King's Road almost immediately bends left, go straight on under the railway bridge and walk along Hurlingham Road. (The entrance to Putney Bridge Underground station is on the right just before Hurlingham Road.) Opposite Foskett Road there's a yellow **'Frisia'** cultivar of **False Acacia**, a **Chusan Palm** in a front garden and, right next to the entrance to Hurlingham Park, another front garden hosts a splendid **Saucer Magnolia**.

Just inside the park turn left through the gate marked by a pair of towering **Hybrid Poplars** into a delightful oval garden where there are several trees to admire.

Dominating the central lawn is a large **'Glauca' Atlas Cedar** with its distinctive blue-grey foliage. Look out too for a thriving **Tulip Tree** and, in the north-east corner, a lovely **Black Mulberry**. Leave this small garden by the gate next to a particularly large **Norway Maple** through to the playing field, with the tennis courts ahead. Every summer polo is also played here, at an exclusive event rather like Henley Regatta with horses.

'Fulham' Oak

Turn left along the roadway, where, tucked away next to a rather dilapidated shed, is the park's most interesting tree. It is, appropriately enough, an example of a rare **'Fulham' Oak**, of which there are less than 100 in existence. It is another cultivar, like the 'Lucombe' oak (see page 59), of the hybrid between Turkey and Cork Oaks. This one originates from Osborne's Nursery, an historic horticultural enterprise based in Fulham, which developed it around 1760.

The Fulham Oak is relatively young, and might be considered a tad underwhelming. But demanding attention from over the ad-joining wall is a large, eye-catching **Cedar of Lebanon**. From here, follow the road out of the park to re-join Hurlingham Road, turning right alongside the row of fine, mature London planes lining its edge.

Cross Broomhouse Road to admire, across the road from Sulivan Primary School, a fine **Nettle Tree**, still quite young,

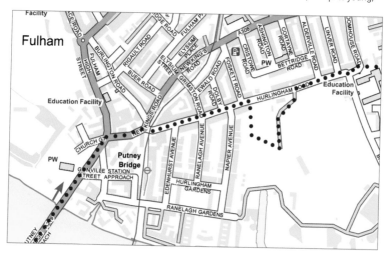

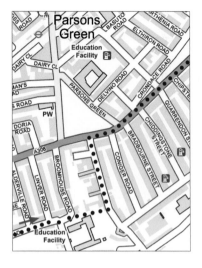

widens, as the pavement becomes a tunnel of plane trees.

Just before the Art Deco Talisman building on the right, take the path on the left towards the main wide-open expanse of Eel Brook Common, next to a pair of particularly straight and smooth trunked planes, suggesting they may be of the **'Augustine Henry'** cultivar. At the end of this short path, a mature **Elm** may cause you to stop: it is one of the Dutch Elm Disease-resistant trees planted since the 1970s, but which one requires specific elm expertise this author sadly lacks. From here take the path off to the right to cross the Common, passing the playground and yet more magnificent **London Planes**.

In the far-right corner follow the path between the black and green railings

but nevertheless one of the older trees of this species in London. At the corner, head down the narrow corridor of Bell's Alley, beneath an amazing column of towering, thinly-pollarded **London Plane** trees, something like the aisle of a Gothic cathedral. At the end turn left into Peterborough Road, pass a trio of **Silver Birches**, and follow it up to Parson's Green, another handsome urban green space. At its centre you may notice a stand of **Raywood Ash** trees – these are particularly noticeable in the autumn as their fine, feathery foliage takes on striking autumn hues. You can see why the seventies pub-rock scene has been supplanted by yummy-mummies and SUVs in this desirably sylvan corner of west London.

Cross over New King's Road and follow it eastwards, to the right, another magnificent line of mature London Plane trees leading the way past the parade of boutiquey shops, soon to reach Eel Brook Common. This begins narrow and gradually

Nettle Tree

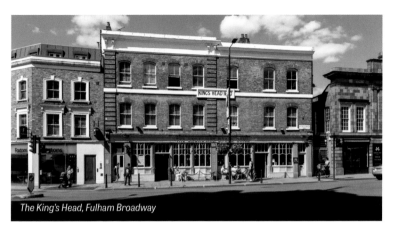

The King's Head, Fulham Broadway

alongside the road, past a semi-derelict terraced area of the park, to emerge on Erin Close by a Boris bikes dock. Then go right on Effie Road and quickly left on Harwood Road to arrive at the main junction and Fulham Broadway with the Broadway Bar opposite. Cross the junction on your left, pausing by the lights to pay homage at McGettigan's. Nowadays an unremarkable bar and grill, it used to be yet another music pub in these parts: the Swan. The publisher of this book will have you know that his first band played their second gig here. (OK, last gig.)

Now we follow Fulham Broadway to the right, past the brown, terracotta-tiled Market Hall (next to another former pub-rock venue, the King's Head), to Fulham Broadway Tube station. Just beyond, a Tree of Heaven marks the corner of Waterford Road.

Continue on past Chelsea's Stamford Bridge football ground, noting the mature **False Acacias** just before its Bovril Gate (does anyone really drink Bovril at Premier League matches? It doesn't seem the obvi-

ous beverage for the executive box). Beyond, a faux-Spanish style doorway with a black wooden door signposted as Chelsea Design Studios has a couple of interesting boughs hanging over its high pantile-topped wall: an Australian **Blackwood** and an **Almond**.

Keep going for a good 500 metres,

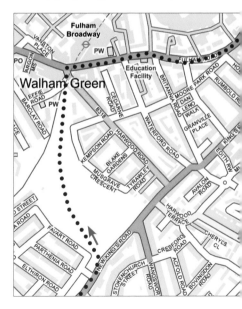

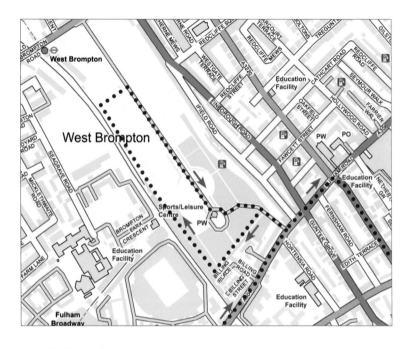

The Man Who Made the Who

looking out for an Esso garage on your right. Here, turn through the gates on your left. This is Brompton Cemetery: not just a vast burial ground for over 200,000 people, but a magnificently verdant Victorian oasis in which to wander. We're going to seek out two graves in particular.

From the entrance take the first path on the left and follow it alongside the cemetery's southern wall for several hundred yards, keeping a look-out for a small silver disc fixed into the path on its left edge, bearing the number 25. Up against the wall beyond it is the Lambert family grave, the headstone commemorating three generations interred here, including two of music. The earlier is Constant Lambert, the early-twentieth-century composer and co-founder of Sadler's Wells Ballet; the latter, which is why we've come to pay our respects, is his son Kit Lambert, the manager of the Who.

This slumbrous spot hardly seems to set the right tone for the younger Lambert, who also deserves a place in posterity for signing Jimi Hendrix to the Track Records label he founded: his short life (drink and drugs did for him, at just 45, the same age as his similarly dissolute father) was as chaotic as you'd expect from the man who presided over an act remembered as one of the most incendiary of their era. But perhaps the riotous foliage all around is appropriate after all: before coming upon the Who Lambert had taken part in an extraordinary expedition to the Brazilian jungle under the explorer John Hemming, which ended with his best friend being killed and scalped by an Amazonian tribe.

The gravestone's epitaph could not be clearer: 'The Man Who Made the Who'. After Pete Townshend had smashed his guitar one night after bashing the ceiling while unwisely waving it above his head, it was Lambert who decided they must destroy their equipment every night. It was Lambert who, noticing that when the band's Mod audience were high on speed they stammered, put the stutter in 'My G-G-Generation'; Lambert who helped Townshend focus his ideas for a rock opera into what became Tommy and eventually got it put on at the Met.

Now follow this path to its end and turn right up the western avenue. Just past the stands of Stamford Bridge to the left and right are several steepling Lombardy-type poplars (most likely **Plantière Poplars**), always breezy and elegant to behold. Look out along the path's left-hand edge for silver disc number 81 – if you reach a right turning with a water tap you've gone slightly too far. Towards the back, behind a sprinkling of neat white headstones of military casualties from the Second World War, is the flat, slate

Plantière Poplars

gravestone of Bernard Levin, the celebrated *Times* columnist, acerbic satirist on *That Was the Week That Was* and scourge of cant and humbug. 'Words have an existence of their own,' reads the epitaph: 'they are not ours to command altogether freely, but without us they cannot come to life.'

But weren't Levin's musical tastes more inclined to Wagner? In 1995 the suicide of Kurt Cobain prompted him to devote his column to an appraisal of Nirvana's *In Utero* and *Nevermind* albums. In comparison with Alfred Brendel's rendition of Beethoven's sonatas he found them wanting: in a year or two, he assured his readers, Cobain's followers would have forgotten all about him.

Brompton Cemetery

Brompton Cemetery is one of London's 'Magnificent Seven' nineteenth-century cemeteries that ring the inner city. Opened to provide dignified burials for the city's growing population, Brompton was laid out as an open-air cathedral, or a 'Garden of Sleep', around a cruciform design.

The Central Avenue leads from the northern entrance to the Great Circle and the domed Chapel towards the southern end at the head of the cross.

Trees were central to the plan, and some of the oldest and most noticeable are the Common Limes that form the Central Avenue, many of which date from soon after the cemetery's opening in 1840. Other limes are here too and, especially round the southern end, some fine examples of weeping **'Petiolaris' Silver Limes**, the oldest of which is thought to have been planted for Queen Victoria's Silver Jubilee in 1862.

Brompton has a rather different feel to the bosky, overgrown tangle of London's other Victorian cemeteries like Highgate and Nunhead, partly because it is still in use, but also because of the sheer number of graves here. But it is still an important semi-natural habitat close to the centre of London, where plants and animals are able to co-exist within a relatively gentle human-made environment.

There are dozens of other trees to marvel at here, many of them dating back over a century. You will notice some fine **Holm Oaks**, and an array of characterful conifers, including several pines, some of which were imported by the Victorians from Poland. Look out too for a mature **Strawberry Tree** and, towards the northern gate, perhaps its rarest tree, an **Oregen Maple**.

And for completists, the other six of the Magnificent Seven are, clockwise from Brompton: Kensal Rise, Highgate, Abney Park, Tower Hamlets, Nunhead and West Norwood.

3 – The King's Road to Margaretta Terrace

London Plane with young Rolling Stones, Chelsea Embankment, 1963

If you fancy a refreshment stop, continue up this path to the end, and the cemetery's attractive café; otherwise return via the Central Avenue and Great Circle to the South Gate you came in by, turn left back onto the main road, and cross over to take the second turning on the right, Edith Grove.

Follow this down to the King's Road, passing, after the Chelsea Baptist Church on the left, a **Sycamore** overhanging the pavement enmeshed with wisteria that from May is resplendent with mauve blossom. Cross over the King's Road, with, on the corner on the right, a fine **Southern Catalpa** with its huge, trowel-shaped leaves that in summer is full of white flowers – and continue down Edith Grove.

Near the bottom, at number 102, is what in 1962 became the Rolling Stones' first flat: the bachelor pad of Mick, Keith and Brian Jones. In those days it had no bathroom, apparently, and when the Beatles were invited back there after a gig at the Crawdaddy Club in Richmond they are said to have been disgusted at its squalor. Keith Richards was later to reminisce with, it sounds, some pride of 'the substances growing out of the crockery, the greasy, cold pans piled in junked pyramids of foulness that no one could bear to touch'.

The **London Plane** trees opposite, in front of the huge redbrick World's End estate, would have been there back then, and aren't London's most pristine specimens either. As we shall see, when the Stones

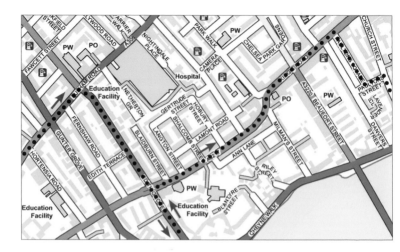

move to the posher part of Chelsea, the plane trees go upmarket too.

Double back up to the King's Road and turn right along it past the World's End pub. Now we come to the long strip of this famous thoroughfare that was as much the stylistic home of the Sixties and Seventies as Carnaby Street. At the corners of many roads off the north side of the Kings Road you will notice **Magnolias** have been planted: Slaidburn and Langton Streets have slow-growing Japanese **Kobushi Magnolias**.

On the left, number 488 (if you didn't know you were in Chelsea you do now: this is a chandelier shop) used to be Granny Takes a Trip, a boutique specialising in retro clothing often with a dandyish, Eastern vibe, that in the mid-sixties would take the fancy of bands like the Stones, in their sitars and Moroccan drummers phase, and Syd Barrett from Pink Floyd: kaftans, velvet loon pants and frilly cuffs. In 1966 Jimi Hendrix kitted himself out here with a vengeance.

There is a T. Rex connection too: one of its frequently changing murals was painted by Mickey Finn, who was later to accompany Marc Bolan on bongo drums.

On the right, opposite Shalcomb Street, there is a **Silver Maple** and a **Weeping Willow** inside the World's End Nursery. Walk up Shalcomb Street, with an evergreen **Southern Magnolia** in a front garden on the corner, complementing another **Kobushi**

Granny Takes a Trip, 1970

tree on the street. You'll see its street trees are planted in opposite pairs, including two Trees of Heaven and, at the corner with Lamont Street, a pair of **Three-lobed**, or **Erect Crabapples**. Turn right on Lamont Street to the corner of Hobury Street – a fine old **Silver Birch** here – where you turn right reaching a very good example of a **Japanese Zelkova** just before the junction with the King's Road, where you turn left once more.

At number 430, with its railway-terminus-size clock, hands spinning maniacally in the wrong direction, is World's End, Vivienne Westwood's emporium. It was a boutique back in the sixties, but its heyday was the seventies. By late 1971, this was Let It Rock, Westwood and Malcolm McLaren's first boutique, which boasted Marc Bolan as an occasional customer for its teddy-boy memorabilia.

In 1972 it had become the James Dean-inspired Too Fast to Live, Too Young to Die, but it was in 1974, rebranded again as Sex, that it started selling torn T-shirts with

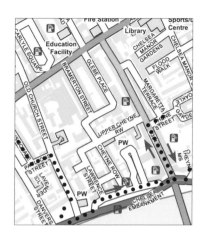

Punk icon Jordan outside Sex

decorative safety pins, and established the uniform that would soon be associated with Punk. Just as crucially, this was where the Sex Pistols met, to be shaped by McLaren's Svengali management into the anarchic shock troops of punk rock.

A little further on, opposite the World's End Bookshop, you'll pass three recently planted **Japanese Pagoda Trees**. Follow the King's Road round, passing a towering **Spaeth's Alder** outside the Bluebird Restaurant. These rare hybrid alders, with cherry-like leaves and cones (a typical alder feature) can be a confusing tree to identify. Now cross over the King's Road and turn right down the eastern (furthest) side of Paultons Square.

This private square hosts a lovely arboreal array, among them an **Almond**, a **Mimosa**, a **Golden Rain Tree** and a **Strawberry Tree**. At its centre a magnificent **Saucer Magnolia**, complemented by a collection of ornamental crabapples and cherries, is resplendent in spring. But perhaps the Square's greatest arboreal prize are the very old **False Acacias** dotted around the perimeter, maybe even as old as the Square itself. The east side of the square once hosted two distinguished literary residents, commemorated with blue plaques – the novelist Jean Rhys and the dramatist Samuel Beckett – while Gavin Maxwell of *Ring of Bright Water* fame resided on the western side.

At the bottom of the square turn left along Paultons Street to Old Church Street, with the Chelsea Pig pub on the corner. Opposite and just to your left is the entrance to the Old Dairy at number 46 – an eighteenth-century building with scrolling gables like something out of a Dutch townscape painting. Painted tiles on the wall illustrate its former function with bucolic views of cows and a pail-carrying milkmaid.

Out of sight around the back used to be Sound Techniques recording studios where, during the sixties and seventies, Pink Floyd recorded 'Arnold Layne' and 'See Emily Play', and the fragile troubadour Nick Drake, a protegé of the influential producer Joe

Monument unveiled at the opening of the Chelsea Embankment

Boyd, recorded all of his albums; Marc Bolan and Tyrannosaurus Rex (the earlier, pre-hits incarnation) also paid a visit.

To your right Old Church Street joins Cheyne Walk beside, on your right as you face the river, sunken Roper's Gardens, which has much to admire. An unfinished stone-relief sculpture by Sir Jacob Epstein is complemented by an old ornamental cherry planted by Gunji Koizumi, who introduced the judo to the UK, and some newly planted **Southern Catalpas**, of the **'Aurea'** cultivar. But most intriguing is a tree that appears to be from the **Walnut** family, with an enigmatic plaque telling us it was 'Planted by Men of the Trees (London Branch), 1965'.

This distinguished street, boasting many fine Jacobean and Queen Anne townhouses, has long been the abode of the great and the good – all the way back to Thomas More in the 1500s – and something

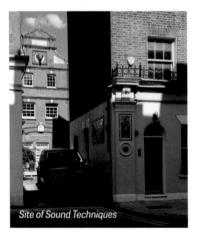
Site of Sound Techniques

of an artists' colony too. Past residents include the painters Turner and Whistler, the composer Vaughan Williams, and writers from T. S. Eliot to Ian Fleming. George Best, who also lived here, qualifies as another kind of artist. What more aspirational address for the upwardly mobile rock aristocracy?

Turn left through the garden in front of Chelsea Old Church just after the monument commemorating the opening of the Chelsea Embankment in 1874, and admire the painted statue of Thomas More on your right, before emerging on Cheyne Walk by a large **Ginkgo**.

A little further along, clambering up the side of the 50 Cheyne restaurant, is an unkempt **Loquat**. It's an interesting choice for a restaurant – maybe the fruit and the leaves, used in a herbal infusion in its native Japan, are on the menu? Cheyne Row to the left leads to the house of Thomas Carlyle, the nineteenth-century writer little read now, but highly regarded during his lifetime; the leonine bust of him opposite may more readily bring to mind Father John Misty.

Now take a left up Oakley Street. This predominantly white stucco-fronted street has both arboreal and rock distinction. It was part of an 1850 development which included the very first street trees in London to be planted, thanks to the eccentric John Phené. These days you'd hardly know it. But opposite a lonely **False Acacia** is its monument to music: a blue plaque at number 42 marks the residence of the great reggae musician Bob Marley.

Marley took up residence here in 1977 after surviving an assassination attempt in Jamaica. During his stay he and his band the Wailers recorded perhaps their most famous studio album, *Exodus*, over at Island Records' studios in Chiswick. More to the point, most days they would go across Albert Bridge and play football in Battersea Park.

If you fancy a refreshment break around here, the Phené pub on Phené Street, just beyond Marley's erstwhile abode, was apparently George Best's favourite for a great many. Just before the pub, look up Margaretta Terrace, part of Phené's development and, towering over the far end of the street, can be seen, just possibly, the only tree – a **London Plane** – surviving from the original planting.

The solitary Margaretta Terrace Plane

4 – Oakley Street to Battersea

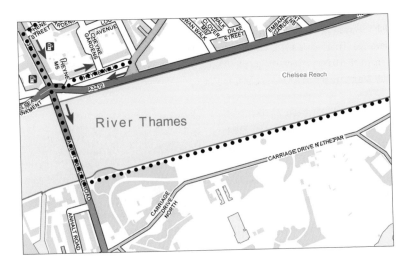

Retrace your steps down Oakley Street, and turn left to walk along the final short stretch of Cheyne Walk. In 1967 Mick Jagger bought number 48 and moved in with Marianne Faithfull. Two years later Keith Richards moved into number 3 (a blue plaque next door commemorates the final, brief residence of the novelist George Eliot) with his girlfriend Anita Pallenberg.

When number 3's previous occupant, the former Conservative minister Sir Anthony Nutting, dropped by one day to pick up any mail, he was startled to find the room where Winston Churchill had dined draped in black and decorated with giant black candlesticks, and an oak-panelled drawing room once privy to discussions of the Suez crisis now hosting a piano in psychedelic livery, a large hookah and a mirror ball.

Since we are on a tree walk, we should note Keith Richards' notorious arboreal encounter in 2006, when his emergency brain surgery forced the cancellation of the Stones' European tour: a mishap improbably attributed to him falling out of a coconut palm in Fiji. 'Keith Richards out of his tree,' mused a correspondent to the *Guardian*'s Letters page: 'that's hardly what you'd call news, is it?'

This final, almost crescent-shaped stretch of Cheyne Walk is screened from the main A320 by Chelsea Embankment Gardens, a delightfully tranquil spot from which to survey the Thames. Before the Gardens and grand plane-lined Chelsea Embankment were constructed in the 1870s, Cheyne Walk was right above the river's high-water mark.

If you want even more arboreal diversity you can cross over from Cheyne Walk to Royal Hospital Road where, a short distance up on the right, is Chelsea Physic

John Samuel Phené

John Samuel Phené was something of a Renaissance man. Architect, antiquarian, developer, Francophile and scholar, he inherited land in Chelsea on which in 1851, he constructed Oakley Street, Margaretta Terrace and Phené Street, along with the Phené pub. Maybe we should add narcissist to the list . . .

This new development of upmarket suburban housing incorporated the latest planning ideas imported from the continent. Phené had spent time in France, where he had been aware of Hausmann's celebrated improvements to Paris. At the heart of the Parisian scheme was the construction of the grands boulevards, replacing the maze-like medieval street plan. But perhaps the most striking feature of the new broad and straight boulevards was their being lined with trees, usually Planes.

Phené determined to implement these continental innovations in burgeoning London. His Chelsea development had trees planted in the pavements on either side of its new streets, a feature quickly admired by many, including Prince Albert, who took a keen interest in planning matters. But for the next twenty years, these three Chelsea streets were the only examples of planned, tree-lined thoroughfares in the capital, until the Victoria Embankment was opened in 1871.

A kind of town-planning equivalent of Nick Drake, Phené's scheme met with critical success, but, ahead of its time, didn't go mainstream until years later.

Unlike Nick Drake, however, Phené lived to the ripe old age of 90, developing a reputation for eccentricity. He built a

George Best's favoured watering hole

five-storey mansion on Upper Cheyne Row where he accumulated a vast collection of ephemera from his world travels. The house became something of a local landmark, and known as the 'Gingerbread Castle'. Like the trees – save for the lone plane on Margaretta Terrace – there is no sign of it now: it was demolished in 1924.

Bob Marley and footballing friends, Battersea Park

Garden. But perhaps that's for another day, so double back to the junction with Oakley Street and cross the river on the left-hand side of Albert Bridge.

This, the last leg of the walk, takes you through one of London's great nineteenth-century parks, designed (along with its twin in East London, Victoria Park) by James Pennethorne. Like the Chelsea Physic Garden, Battersea Park could warrant an entire chapter of this book, so in order to get to the north-east corner, a simple route is described here.

Enter the Park by the first gate on your left, and turn left past a young native **Black Poplar**, a stone plaque telling us it was planted in 2012. Hundreds of years ago, huge Black Poplars would have been a frequent sight along the Thames. Now they are one of our rarest trees, thanks to centuries of human development destroying their natural habitat of estuarine floodplains.

Keep straight ahead on the riverside terrace, with the main bulk of the park on your right. Fine views of the Chelsea Embankment across the river can be enjoyed, while noting the irrepressible saplings growing out of the park's own riverside wall. Mostly these are **Sycamore**, but several self-sown **London Plane** seedlings can be seen clinging on to what may constitute their ideal environment – dry, with plenty of

reflected heat, and occasional drenching when the tide rises high enough.

At the end of the riverside walkway, the path leads round under Chelsea Bridge to take you through the new estate of riverside apartment blocks. From here, follow Pump House Lane around to Battersea Power Station Tube station (opening in autumn 2021), or for Battersea Park National Rail Station, head back to Sopwith Way to the west of Grosvenor Railway Bridge, and follow it round to join Queenstown Road.

Turn left on Queenstown Road, passing some multi-stemmed **Trident Maples** and a **Field Maple** on the corner of Sopwith Way, and follow it over Queen's Circus with the south-eastern Rosery Gate to Battersea Park on your right, and then turn left on Battersea Park Road to reach the station.

But there is one last music landmark here we can't miss even if we tried. Dominating the skyline a lot less since the building of all these vast ramparts of flats around it (even if to pay for its restoration) is the Thirties architectural masterpiece of Battersea Power Station. It deserves attention on this walk for one reason: in December 1976 locals were astonished to see a giant inflatable pink pig rising between the power station's four fluted chimneys.

This was Pink Floyd's doing: by now no longer the trippy, whimsical outfit that nearly a decade earlier had recorded in Old Church Street but one of the biggest rock acts of all time, they wanted a commensurately epic cover shot for their new album *Animals*. The potential hazard a 30-foot pink pig could pose to air traffic was prudently insured against by employing a marksman to

shoot it down if it broke free of its moorings, but the photoshoot went into a second day, the marksman wasn't kept on, and the pig's inevitable bid for freedom saw it last sighted over Chatham in Kent.

Where the pink pig flew

Horse Chestnuts on Ealing Common

How the Elephant Got Its Trunk

Acton to Ealing

Was it true, as I had heard, that in Ealing there was an
elephant buried beneath an oak tree?
The quest took me on a fascinating wander through leafy
west London that took in dozens of arboreal curiosities and
two truly great trees, as well as the typical flora of London's
more affluent suburbs. I should have known: the clues, I
discovered, were in the names: Acton derives from 'Ac', an
old English word for Oak, and Ealing has long been
crowned the 'Queen of the Suburbs'.
This route takes in many lovely, venerable trees
on a long-established village green, the expanse of Ealing
Common and a historic Georgian park landscape. Fine
Edwardian architectural detailing in Acton, substantial villas in
Ealing and a Grade I-listed manor house are all included.

Length: 5 miles (10,000 steps)
Start: Acton Central (Overground)
Finish: Ealing Broadway (District and Central Lines, Elizabeth Line (late 2021),
National Rail)
Shortening: Ealing Common Tube station (District and Picadilly Lines)
Accessibility: Pavements and level surfaces, crossing some busy roads and some
unmade paths
Relative Difficulty: 2/5

1 – Acton Central to Uxbridge Road

From Acton Central Overground Station, turn left along Churchfield Road (if you have arrived on the westbound platform, you will need to make your way over the level crossing).

Subtropical Acton

Turn right after 70 metres onto the delightful-sounding Myrtle Road. Sadly, no Myrtles can be seen on this street, but after a **Bastard Service Tree**, a characterful old Sycamore hangs over it on the corner of Chaucer Road. This elderly but rather small Sycamore is the main attraction of a charming pocket park. It is unclear whether the park appeared out of a bomb site or other such catastrophe, or whether it has been a vacant plot since the houses were built. Either way, it's a delightful community space that brightens up this corner and, while not far into this route, offers the potential for respite.

Continue on Myrtle Road until its small street trees are replaced by mature **Common Limes**. The street name changes too: now you are on the far more upmarket-sounding Cumberland Park. A substantial house just before Woodhurst Road (where you turn left) has a back garden that may catch your eye. It is something of a tropical oasis: **Chusan Palms**, **Tree Ferns** and **Banana** plants can be glimpsed over its high brick walls.

After a short distance, turn right off Woodhurst Road on Maldon Road, graced with a couple of large and mature **'Fastigiata' Hornbeams**. At the end turn left on

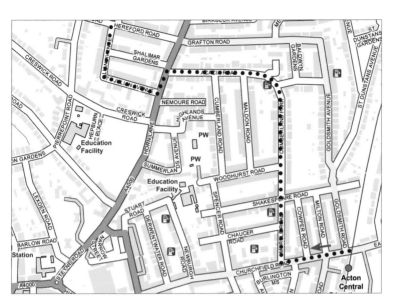

Acacia Road, a street that one might reasonably expect to be lined with **False Acacias**, a species that was a frequent choice in decades past – the 'Acacia' of suburban street names often refers to it. But there is no sign of any Acacia here now, save for a lone tree, possibly of the dense-canopied **'Umbraculifera'** cultivar, in a front garden on the right towards the Horn Lane junction.

Honey Locust leaves

At Horn Lane, cross and turn left briefly before taking a right on Julian Avenue, marked by a large **Honey Locust** on the right. A little further along on the left-hand side, a mature **Pedunculate Oak** blocks half the pavement. Unusually, it is planted on the inner side of the pavement, forcing pedestrians closer to the roadway, suggesting that it was not planted as a street tree. It is conceivable that it pre-dates the street, and was left in situ as a landmark from a previous landscape. Continue straight ahead until the road curves round by a young **Chinese Tree Privet**. Behind you, an unnamed road leads into the grounds of some flats, where you'll see a huge old **Holm Oak**.

As Julian Avenue curves, another large **Honey Locust** (a tree much favoured in these parts) appears, and beyond on the right a dramatic sight opens up – a huge conifer seemingly growing in the middle of

Swamp Cypress

the road. If you are following this route in the winter, you may be even more surprised, as it is a deciduous **Swamp Cypress**, and its silhouette is not that of a typical rocket-shaped conifer.

This multi-stemmed giant is an anomaly. Like the oak round the corner, it has been built around, and is now a remarkable traffic-calmer protected by a semi-circular build-out from the pavement. According to locals, it is a remnant from the gardens of a former country estate, Shalimar, which gave its name to Shalimar Gardens, a turning off Julian Avenue. The houses appear to be Edwardian, so the tree must have been already significant over 100 years ago. Perhaps it is 200 years old – it certainly has the girth of an old tree.

At the end of Julian Avenue, just after an elegant **Japanese Zelkova**, turn left on Hereford Road, where you'll find another oak also, like the Swamp Cypress, jutting out into the road. Behind some flats the unmistakable flat-top of a **Cedar of Lebanon** can be seen – maybe both these trees are

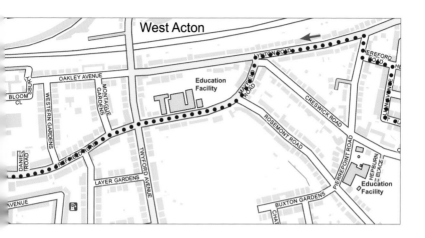

West Acton

remnants of the former estate. At the end of Hereford Road, turn right onto Pierrepoint Road, adorned with **Common Limes**, and on the left there is a **Small-leaved Lime**, one of the parent species of the hybrid Common Lime, to compare. You may notice the Small-leaved tree actually has similarly sized leaves to its hybrid progeny, but Common Limes are altogether more vigorous, producing much suckering of shoots around the base. They're favoured by honeydew-secreting aphids too.

Next, turn left on broad Lynton Road until you reach the junction of Mayfield Road. Turn left past an ornate lamp post, while noting a fastigiate **Cypress Oak** planted on the pavement in Creswick Road. These streets are wide, but relatively unplanted, making walking them less pleasant than shadier, more densely street-tree-planted thoroughfares. It appears the scourge of the suburbs is to blame: off-street parking, and its demand for easy access across pavements unobstructed by trees. Follow Mayfield Road round as it turns into Creffield

Road with, thankfully, more tree cover.

On your right, a low brick wall marks the playing field of the Japanese School. As the buildings appear, there is a **Goat Willow**, followed by several other trees including a couple of maturing Asian **Magnolias**. But beyond the main gate, the school's most interesting tree can be seen. It is a **'Baobab' Plane**, a rare cultivar of London Plane with

'Baobab' Plane bole

Deodar Cedar

quite distinctive characteristics, most conspicuously a great swollen bole. They are an altogether smaller, some might say sickly-looking tree, with twisted, pendulous branches and leaves more deeply incised than most London Planes. They appear to have arisen in the nineteenth century, and all the known trees – of which there can be less than 100 in the UK, mostly in London – are at least 100 years old.

Some think their strange appearance is due to an infection, but as they are all roughly the same age, and all appear to have been specifically planted, they are more likely a long-forgotten cultivar, or variety, of London Plane. For comparison, a more usual form of **London Plane** can be seen across the street.

Beyond the school, the trees start to become sparser as the driveways to concreted-over front gardens resume. As you cross Twyford Avenue, Acton becomes Ealing, and the houses become grander as Creffield Road continues.

After 400 metres, you can turn left on Wolverton Gardens to shorten the route at Ealing Common Tube station. Otherwise, follow it for another 200 metres until you reach a modern hotel building on the left, next to which is a towering **Deodar Cedar**. This is a branch of the Doubletree chain, which is surely a sign that another interesting tree must lurk nearby . . .

Sure enough, when you follow the hotel round on to Uxbridge Road, on the corner with Gunnersbury Avenue leading through Ealing Common is a splendid **Oriental Plane**.

Swamp Cypress

Taxodium distichum

Swamp Cypresses are part of a rare band: deciduous conifers. Among that exclusive group they are perhaps the least planted. Of the others, the larches, while unusual in London, are frequent in more northerly and western parts of the UK, and the one other often found in London, Dawn Redwood, is easily confused with Swamp Cypress.

Swamp Cypress has been here for centuries, having been introduced from the south-east United States by the famous gardener, plantsman and Lambeth-dweller John Tradescant the elder sometime in the early 1600s. The oldest individual tree in the UK is known to have been planted in 1750 at Syon House, and in its native US the species can live for thousands of years. Upstart Dawn Redwoods, on the other hand, have only been with us for about 70 years (see page 91).

In their natural habitat, Swamp Cypresses are found in damp and frequently flooded places, but they are quite tolerant of drier locations too. Acton, for instance. If you find one growing near water, look out for the 'knees': woody root growths that sometimes emerge near the main trunk. It was once thought the knees helped the trees breath in waterlogged conditions, but now research suggests their purpose is to provide stability in soft ground.

They are at their most dramatic in the autumn when their leaves – or needles – start to turn fabulous shades of gold, orange and chestnut brown before they fall, leaving the trees bare through the winter. If your tree is big and old, then it's likely to be a Swamp Cypress, but a close look at the needles is the surest way to tell if you are dealing with a Swamp Cypress rather than a Dawn Redwood. The needles of a Swamp Cypress are held alternately along the stem, while those of Dawn Redwoods are opposite.

2 – Ealing Common to Pitzhanger Manor

From the Uxbridge Road, you need to get across the busy roads in front of you in order to traverse the Common beyond. From the Oriental Plane, turn off Uxbridge Road onto Gunnersbury Avenue leading through the Common extension until you reach the North Circular Road and a crossing at the traffic lights.

Once over the North Circular (at its least ferocious here in Ealing), you should make your way across the Common, heading for its south-west corner. Warwick Road offers a pleasant **Horse Chestnut**-lined route to your destination, but you may want to head off piste and across the great grassy expanse of the Common.

At the end of Warwick Road, the enclosed Warwick Dene is on your left, and, across the road is the Grange, a Youngs pub offering a tempting interruption. Turning right here on the Common, look out for an **Indian Horse Chestnut** tucked among the

Indian Horse Chestnut

regular Horse Chestnuts, noticeable for later flowering and more slender leaves. It is the horse chestnut species now favoured, as it is not subject to the disfiguring leaf miner attack that turns our traditional European horse chestnuts brown in summer.

A little further along, turn right onto Grange Park, which after 50 metres ends at a triangle of greenery notable for a **Red Horse Chestnut** where the road forks. Take the right fork and then turn onto Grange Park, past a mature **Holly** and a pair of **False Acacias**, with an **Erman's Birch** in front of you on the opposite pavement. This is very much comfortable Victorian Ealing, typified by large houses and a vaguely village-like feel, despite the proximity of the North Circular.

At the end of Grange Park, turn left onto Grange Road, marked by a multi-stemmed Sycamore on the corner. Substantial Victorian houses and later mansion blocks of flats, where once even grander houses stood, line this street. As in Acton, many former front gardens have become car parks, but there are still some handsome trees remaining from more glorious days.

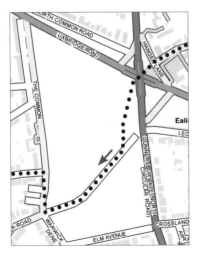

Horse Chestnut avenue, Ealing Common

Look out for old limes, horse chestnuts and cedars, but the most unusual tree along here is a large fastigiate **Elm**, which despite its size is perhaps just 40 years old, a new Dutch Elm Disease-resistant variety, maybe the **'Columella'** cultivar.

Continue on Grange Road for about 300 metres to reach Ealing Green, a busy road with the sliver of the Green across the street. Turn right where a **Copper Beech** towers over a brick wall on your right, until you reach the Grove pub, where traffic lights allow you to cross and enter the Green.

Ealing Green is a genteel nineteenth-century place shaded by a canopy of aged **London Planes**. Follow the lane that cuts across to Ealing College, noticing a particularly burred and voluminous plane on the right. Just beyond this lovely old tree, turn right on the path beyond taking you past Ealing Studios. These are the oldest film production studios in the world, where classic post-war Ealing Comedies, including *Passport to Pimlico* and *Kind Hearts and Coronets*, were filmed. The studios are still in use today with the likes of *Shaun of the Dead* and *Downton Abbey* among more recent productions.

After the studios, a semi-circular war memorial flanks the main entrance to Ealing's finest building, Pitzhanger Manor, the country home of architect Sir John Soane.

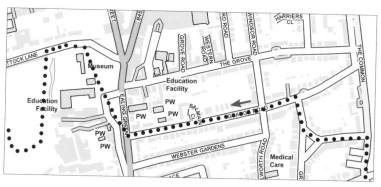

Sir John Soane and Pitzhanger Manor

Sir John Soane (1753–1837) is remembered as one of the most important architects of his generation, responsible for a slew of stately homes and churches. His greatest achievements, though, are considered to be the Bank of England, Dulwich Picture Gallery and his London home in Lincoln's Inn Fields, now the Sir John Soane's Museum (see page 194).

Pitzhanger Manor

After initially struggling to establish his practice in the 1780s, Soane landed a plum job as architect and surveyor to the Bank of England, a position he would keep for decades and which paid a percentage of the value of all the building work he undertook. Over the years he completely remodelled the Bank. Other lucrative positions came his way, including Clerk of Works at the Royal Hospital Chelsea, and a similar position at the Palace of Westminster, and he was even appointed Deputy Surveyor of His Majesty's Woods and Forests.

By 1800, Soane had become both highly successful and very wealthy. He had amassed an enviable collection of art, antiquities and curiosities at his London town house, and felt that a country home was required for his family and his collection. It was also to be a showcase for his architectural skills and the location for a dynasty of Soane architects. So in that year he acquired Pitzhanger Manor, an existing country house with considerable grounds in rural Ealing – then, along with Acton, the location of many country seats.

He set about reconfiguring the house, completing it in 1804, but his wife, Eliza, was not keen on Ealing's quiet life and his wayward sons were clearly not going to fulfil his dynastic ambitions. In 1810, therefore, Soane sold Pitzhanger, having barely lived in it. Eventually, Ealing Council acquired the estate in 1900, opening the gardens to the public in 1901 as Walpole Park, named after the last owner, Sir Spencer Walpole, and turning the Manor into the borough's lending library.

After several transformations and uses since, the Manor lost its 'Z', becoming Pitshanger Manor, and eventually shutting for extensive restoration in 2015. It reopened to the public as the restored Pitzhanger Manor and exhibition venue in 2019, revealing Sir John Soane's original architectural vision. The restoration not only included the recovery of the 'Z', but also the opening of a fine museum shop and the establishment of two eateries, one of which, Pitzhanger Pantry, can be accessed from Walpole Park.

3 – Walpole Park to Ealing Broadway

From the war memorial, follow the path round to join Mattock Lane past a bronze-foliaged **Japanese Maple** and a **Tree of Heaven** to the original Soane- designed gateway into the Manor. This grand arch is topped either side by stone caps utilising a design motif of a low dome cut as if with a square die. Similar Soanic finials can be found gracing Dulwich Picture Gallery and Soane's own grave in St Pancras Old Church. It is said that these were the inspiration for Giles Gilbert Scott's design for the classic red telephone box.

Beyond the gateway, follow the wall past a **Horse Chestnut** and, just after, turn left into Walpole Park, to reveal a magnificent park. Mostly contemporary with Soane's Pitzhanger Manor, it was landscaped by

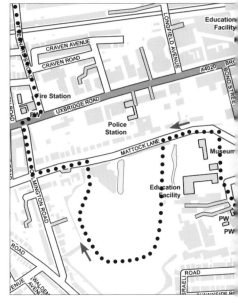

Walpole Park

The rear of Pitzhanger Manor flanked by Cedars of Lebanon

John Haverfield, a head gardener at Kew, but retains a few earlier features. From the entrance follow the path south, keeping the lake on your left. A splendid view of the rear of Pitzhanger Manor opens up, framed by two eighteenth-century **Cedars of Lebanon**.

As you approach the Pitzhanger Pantry, turn left under an avenue of **Common Limes** and **Horse Chestnuts**, with a children's playground on your left. A little way along, a twisted and very characterful tree appears: a **Sweet Chestnut**. Like the Cedars, this tree dates back to the eighteenth century. Continue along the avenue past another water feature, where the path divides; take the slight right turn towards a **Giant Redwood**. Beyond the Redwood, keep straight on towards the exit, stopping to admire an exotic, although slightly dog-eared, grouping of **Cabbage Palms** surrounding a **Monkey Puzzle**.

The gate takes you back onto Mattock Lane, where you turn left, passing a fine example of a **Rowan**, a species much planted in London despite its propensity for wetter and cooler climes, a predilection that often leads to trees ailing after only a decade or two. Continue along the wide grass verge, where you will see a pair of **Dawn Redwoods** to compare with the Julian Avenue Swamp Cypress. After these, turn

Scots Pine

right on Culmington Road, marked by a **Deodar Cedar** in a front garden, and a mature **London Plane** on the left corner. A couple of newly planted **Honey Locusts** adorn this street, but otherwise it is mostly devoid of trees for nearly 100 metres before it meets Uxbridge Road.

Turn right, admiring the stone clad Art Deco fire station on the opposite side of this busy road, with a pair of old **False Acacias** to its left. Cross at the lights and double back towards the fire station, turning right on St Leonard's Road just before it. Continue for about 250 metres, crossing the railway line and eventually reaching a junction marked by a mini-roundabout and a small spinney of **Monterey Cypresses** on the left. Cross straight over and fork right just beyond the junction with Gordon Road onto **London Plane** tree-lined Carlton Road.

Carlton Road is the edge of Ealing's desirable Castlebar neighbourhood, and the houses shaded by the mature planes and limes along here tend to be large and

detached, many with large trees in their gardens. As the road curves round, pause to admire the fine orange-barked **Scots Pine** in Pinewood Grove, along with a shapely **Tree of Heaven** a little further up on the left. Longfield Walk on the right is a mostly Lime-tree-lined walk leading into Ealing town centre; however, the first few trees are rather dull **Chonosuki Crabapples**.

The *pièce de résistance* of Carlton Road, and indeed of this route, is the hulking great **Pedunculate Oak** right in the middle of the road straight ahead. Known as the 'Carlton Road Oak', and by some as the 'Elephant Tree', it marks the spot where, legend has it, an elephant is buried.

The tree is a local landmark and, judging by its appearance, something of an obstacle too. Its trunk shows signs of having been whitewashed in the past, no doubt in an attempt to make it more conspicuous to speeding motorists, some of whom, it seems, may have had a tussle with the tree, which sports a few battle scars. Take the

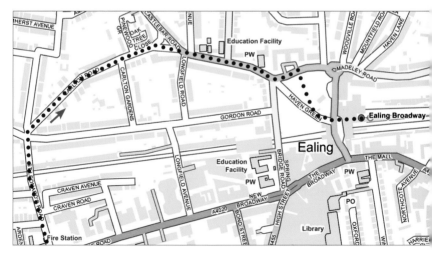

Ealing's Elephant Tree

Barnum and Bailey's Circus elephants plodding through Chesterfield (not Ealing) in 1899

Back in the days when any self-respecting circus had a menagerie of badly-treated animals as part of its entertainment, great processions of clowns, acrobats, caged tigers, feather-adorned horses and semi-comatose elephants would progress slowly through towns and cities drumming up business before they pitched their big top in the local park.

And so it was back in 1889, as a circus was trooping down Castlebar Road, when one of its four-legged stars expired. Being of such bulk, the deceased animal was buried on the spot by the junction with Carlton Road, and subsequently the myth arose of the oak marking its grave.

The Elephant Tree, or the 'Carlton Road Oak', and the three other oaks on the verge just across the road appear to be far older, perhaps 300 years or so, and their position in a row of four suggests they may have formed a boundary, now long forgotten.

So, the Elephant Tree must have been here when the circus was passing all those years ago, and such a memorable event as the death of an elephant on an Ealing street has been conflated with an equally memorable tree that also happens to grow in the middle of an Ealing street, into a single super animal-arboreal memorial.

But how did the tree, elephantine in appearance, come to be in the middle of the road? If it is part of a boundary row, it could be that a lane always went past it, and even forked at the grassy triangle known as Tortoise Green (what might be buried here?), but perhaps in the past the tree was not dislocated from the Green. It's likely that road widening over the years has resulted in its isolation, along with its rather diminished canopy and swollen and battered trunk. It is remarkable that the tree has survived in this position, not only because of the knocks it has sustained, but also because of the pollution and the compaction of the ground around it.

Wouldn't it be wonderful if the road could be narrowed to a single fork at this junction? Or, better still, blocked altogether – the residents of Carlton Road would surely appreciate the lower levels of traffic that would result in it becoming a cul-de-sac?

Southern Magnolia flower

The Elephant Tree, aka the Carlton Road Oak

right fork past Tortoise Green and the other three veteran oaks, all of which have finer silhouettes than their dislocated sibling, no doubt because of the relative safety of their positions.

Continue along Castlebar Road, passing a huge Eucalypt on the corner of Longfield Road. Other trees to look out for in the gardens along here include a yellow-leaved **'Frisia' False Acacia** and a **Caucasian Wingnut**. As Castlebar Road approaches Haven Green, cross over and follow the road past Haven Green Court, an impressive 1930s mansion block. Just beyond, a row of early-nineteenth- century villas appear, where an enormous evergreen **Southern Magnolia** can be seen.

At the lights, cross, and follow the path through the Green which deposits you on the road, also known as Haven Green, by a pair of **Austrian Pines**, one considerably larger than the other. Cross over to a third **Austrian Pine**, and turn left to the forecourt of Ealing Broadway Station, 50 metres ahead, in front of a nondescript 1970s office block.

Looking past a Spaeth's Alder to the Cheapside Plane

The Green Corners
of the City

A St Paul's Perambulation

The City has been in a perpetual cycle of destruction
and reconstruction over the last 2,000 years, so you may be
surprised to discover what grows amid this warren
of ancient and modern.

This short walk takes in some of the Square Mile's
hidden green corners and arboreal highlights. Layers of
development are revealed: the City's changing functions,
its rapid evolution, as well as constants like its evocative
place names and centuries-old trees. To walk around it is to
understand that, despite the privations of limited space and
poor soil (an accumulation of countless generations
of rubble, refuse and human burials), trees do well here.
In fact, they thrive in the man-made environment of
glass and concrete, which contributes to the mild, human-
influenced climate in a phenomenon known as the
'Urban Heat Island Effect'.

Length: 1.5 miles (3,000 steps)
Start and Finish: St Paul's Tube station (Central Line)
Accessibility: Pavements and level surfaces, crossing some busy roads and some
steps in some of the parks and gardens
Relative Difficulty: 1/5

I – St Paul's to the Cheapside Plane

Arriving at St Paul's Tube station take Exit 2 on to Newgate Street with the Cathedral – where you're heading – behind you. Turn around to head down pedestrianised Panyer Alley, keeping an octagonal office building to your left.

American Sweetgums and Spaeth's Alders line Cheapside

After a few metres a piazza opens up with a **'New Horizon' Elm** to your side, a tree dwarfed by the enormous London Planes beyond the black metal railings of St Paul's Churchyard. Follow the railings around to the churchyard entrance on the corner of New Change.

You have entered one of the City's largest green spaces, surrounding the eastern end of Sir Christopher Wren's baroque masterpiece, St Paul's Cathedral. The trees in here are just as exceptional as the architecture. To start with, the **London Planes** are huge: some of the largest, and maybe oldest, in London, their size emphasised

by the confined space in which they grow. But while these giants impress, there are other trees to seek out too. Straight ahead, a curious **Weeping White Mulberry** may be overlooked, especially as beyond it is a shapely, mature **Ginkgo** with a slightly sickly **Grand Fir** next to it, apparently the largest of its type in London.

Follow the path round to the left, passing the fir and a **Judas Tree** beyond, and continue around the east end of the Cathedral. Beyond a **Dawn Redwood** and a **Tree of Heaven**, you will notice a small, silver-foliaged **Willow-leaved Pear** as the southern exit gate comes into view.

Just after a spreading **American Sweetgum**, take a detour down the right fork in the path to find more unusual trees, and one of St Paul's most notable. Another fine **Ginkgo** is on your left, followed, just after a modernist sculpture of Thomas Becket, by a **Strawberry Tree** and, on your right, a rare **Japanese Bitter Orange**.

But the finest sight is a huge **American Sweetgum**, nestled in a corner between the walls of the south transept and the choir. It is surely the largest Sweetgum in the Square Mile, despite being only 70 years old at most. If you continue along this path to its end, you will also see a subtly variegated **'Aureomarginata' Tulip Tree** on your left.

Once you have inspected these trees, double back in order to exit via the gate with a **Cypress Oak** and the formal Festival Gardens on your left. Turn right, hugging the cathedral until you cross the busy road (also named St Paul's Churchyard), with the south transept behind you. Ahead is an arresting view down Peter's Hill and straight over the Millennium Bridge to Tate Modern on the South Bank, with unmistakable **Ginkgo** silhouettes framing it to the right.

Turn left past a low-domed **Ash** tree until you reach the St Lawrence Jewry Memorial Drinking Fountain, an ornate Gothic affair originally located outside the Guildhall. Turn left here on Old Change Court to admire a North American **Pin Oak** with its spiky leaves just before the steps. Return to the drinking fountain and turn right along Cannon Street, passing a row of **Italian Alders**, before turning right on treeless Distaff Lane, with the stone and glass of St Nicholas Cole Abbey at its end.

As the lane curves right, remain on the pavement which slopes down, as Old Fish Street Hill, to the left of the church, where its junction with Queen Victoria Street is marked by a **Honey Locust**. The church also houses the very good Wren Café, presumably named for the church's architect, but confusingly it uses an image of the small

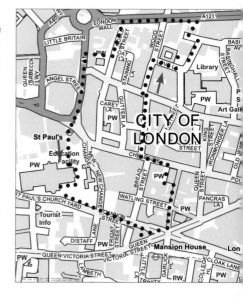

bird in its logo.

Turn left along Queen Victoria Street before crossing just before Friday Street to examine the saplings in front of the new office building on its south side. You'll find a mixed planting of unusual maples, including, most conspicuously, a variegated **Box Elder**, possibly of the **'Flamingo'** cultivar, a small multi-stemmed **Paperbark Maple** and a couple of **Snakebark Maples**.

There are several species of Snakebark Maples, all with striking green bark with white, grey or pink stripes (which must have reminded some archaic tree-namer of snakeskin). Most are Asian, but one species, **Moosewood**, is from North America. These saplings could be that species, but snakebarks are notoriously difficult to tell apart. If any maple experts following this walk can make a positive identification, the author would be interested to know.

Snakebark Maple bark

American Sweetgum

Liquidamber styraciflua

American Sweetgums have been planted a lot in London in recent years. They are handsome trees, with leaves that could be mistaken for a plane or a maple. Like a Sycamore or a Norway Maple, they have five-pointed palmate leaves, and like a plane they produce seedballs.

The St Paul's American Sweet...

autumnal colour.

The St Paul's Churchyard specimen is enormous, and gives a sense of how large these trees can become. It was planted some time after the Second World War, proving that growth can be rapid too. Most trees in London are young – less than 20 years old – those on the north side of Cheapside were planted just a decade ago and are typical of recent street plantings.

They originate from the southern US, where they favour swampy ground and can reach a staggering 45 metres. For comparison, our tallest planes top out at a mere 40 metres, so in favourable locations Sweetgums might one day give them a run for their money.

But Sweetgums have been with us for hundreds of years, and there are few notable individuals around, so it seems those dizzying American heights are unlikely to be reached. Sweetgums also tend to take on a slimmer form than our expansive planes, and are a relatively shorter-lived plant.

Unlike the other species', those leaves are fragrant when crushed, but Sweetgums' most distinctive feature is their autumn leaf display. They turn a range of head-turning hues from gold to vermillion; indeed, they are one of the most reliable big trees for

The scale of recent planting is unprecedented, however, and it will certainly be interesting to see how Sweetgums compare with London Planes in their long-term influence on the cityscape, and how far they enter our affections.

At the end of this planting scheme, pass through the gate into one of the City's delightful parklets, Cleary Garden, a popular and tranquil lunch stop. The garden is on several levels, but the botanical interest can be admired without needing to negotiate any steps. The garden remembers the forward-thinking property developer Fred Cleary (1905–84), celebrated for balancing the urge to build with conserving and creating green spaces. The garden is notable for a luxurious Wisteria and a grape vine and, from an arboreal perspective, a dazzling **'Frisia' False Acacia** and examples of both **Swamp Cypress** and **Dawn Redwoods**, two deciduous conifers easy to confuse.

From the Cleary Garden, continue east along Queen Victoria Street until you reach the crossroads with Cannon Street. Here, cross over both streets, passing Mansion House Tube station and elegant 30 Cannon Street, a 1970s office building originally built for the French bank Crédit Lyonnais, and make for pedestrianised Bow Lane. After a few metres, the narrow lane widens, with the precinct of St Mary Aldermary church on the right, which has been planted with a Ginkgo, and a fine **'Digitata' Oriental Plane**.

Follow Bow Lane as it crosses Watling Street, their narrowness and meagre sunlight stirring a sense of medieval claustrophobia. As Bow Lane approaches Cheapside, turn left into a short passage which opens onto Bow Churchyard, a piazza in the shadow of St Mary-le-Bow church. Listen out for the peel of Bow Bells beneath the churchyard's magnificent **London Plane**.

Leave Bow Churchyard to turn left on Cheapside, lined with thriving street trees.

On the southern, shadier side they are **Spaeth's Alders**, while the northern pavement is planted with **American Sweetgums**. The trees were planted a mere ten years ago, but are thriving, and the Alders in particular are growing apace. But even these young upstarts have some way to go before they can catch up with the huge canopy that can be seen hanging over the street a little further along, where you should make for. This is the Cheapside Plane, a landmark **London Plane** that has been here for many, many years. Cross Cheapside and turn right on Wood Street to take a closer look.

The Cheapside Plane

The Cheapside Plane

The Cheapside Plane actually grows on Wood Street, in the former churchyard of St Peter Cheap, along with 37 others, a church that was not rebuilt after the Great Fire of 1666. It is now one of the City's shadiest pocket parks, as a result of the huge plane that dominates the space.

The Cheapside Plane in the first half of the nineteenth century

It is an old tree: just how old is unclear, but a photograph of its trunk – looking as large as it does today – appears in a book, London Trees, of 1920 confirming that a century ago it was already a landmark. The low-rise shops facing Cheapside over which it hangs testify to its importance too. They are older than many of the buildings in these parts, and show how room for the tree to grow has been prioritised over the development of what must be prime real estate.

So just how old is the Cheapside Plane? It's difficult to say, but just maybe it was planted sometime in the eighteenth century following the great rebuilding of London after the Great Fire of 1666. In his poem, 'The Reverie of Poor Susan', of 1797, William Wordsworth immortalised the location:

At the corner of Wood Street, when daylight appears,
Hangs a Thrush that sings loud, it has sung for three years:
Poor Susan has passed by the spot, and has heard
In the silence of morning the song of the Bird.

Could Wordsworth's thrush have been sat in the Cheapside Plane? There are other old planes in London, the oldest of which is known to have been planted in the 1680s, while others date from the 1770s. The Cheapside Plane is not as huge as the seventeenth-century tree, but it could be eighteenth-century. The huge planes in St Paul's are old too – perhaps as old or even older – but alas they are undated too.

2 – Wood Street to St Paul's

Little else grows in the small, damp and very shady pocket park of St Peter Cheap's tiny churchyard, but an antipodean **Tree Fern** is a valiant exception. Continue north on Wood Street once you have paid your respects.

After about 100 metres you are obliged to cross Gresham Street in a dogleg in order to reach its northern extension. Ahead, the tower of St Alban Wood Street acts as a Gothic landmark dwarfed by the canyon of modern office buildings that surround it. The tower, now a private residence, is all that remains of a Wren church destroyed in the Blitz. A thriving **Nettle Tree** can be seen at its base.

Just before the tower, turn right on Love Lane past the modernist palazzo of Wood Street Police Station – London's finest copshop – until you reach another City parklet, St Mary Aldermanbury, the site of yet another ex-church. Look out for a splendid **Southern Magnolia** and a **Copper Beech** along with the memorial to Henry Condell and John Heminges, actors and parishioners of the church who were instrumental in publishing Shakespeare's First Folio. Across the road from the Gardens, as Love Lane curves into Aldermanbury, there is a splendid **Judas Tree** which has particularly vibrant magenta flowers in May.

Follow Aldermanbury until it curves right into Basinghall Street. Turn left here into Aldermanbury Square, a piazza planted with **Himalayan Birches** and intriguing, high-maintenance 'Parasol Planes'. These are **London Planes** trained to form circular canopies radiating branches akin to a par-

Judas Tree

asol (or, on a rainy day, an umbrella). Leave the square by the passage, Brewers' Hall Garden, to the right of Brewers' Hall. Home to the Worshipful Company of Brewers and established since the 1400s, their hall is a post-war reconstruction of a seventeenth-century building, itself reconstructed after the Great Fire. The passage emerges by a pair of **Honey Locusts** on busy London Wall, where you turn left.

Continue under the Sir Terry Farrell-designed Alban Gate, a postmodern office block, crossing the top end of Wood Street, where you can see **European Alders** on the left and a young **Beech** on the north side of the tower of St Alban. Beyond the junction is the glass and steel building known as 88 Wood Street, designed by the Richard Rogers Partnership. With its brightly coloured, steam ship-inspired heating outlets it is reminiscent of Rogers' famous Centre Pompidou in Paris. More **Honey Locusts** and a **False Acacia** (with pinnate leaves composed of slightly rounder leaflets) surround it, along with a fine **Pedunculate Oak** in the garden of St Olave Silver Street, the site of a church not rebuilt after the Great Fire.

Take a short detour left on Noble Street to admire the ruins of London's Roman Wall, once the north-eastern edge of Londinium. It was uncovered following bomb damage during the Second World War. Back on London Wall, continue past a series of **Chinese Red Birches** opposite the Museum of London. This species is very similar to the white-barked Himalayan Birch, but can be distinguished by the flaking reddish-brown bark of younger branches. Stairs and a walkway on the corner lead to the Museum, a recommended refreshment stop until the Museum relocates to Smithfield.

London Wall turns into Aldersgate as this route skirts the Museum's brick traffic-island edifice, and then once you turn left you are on St Martin's Le Grand. After a few metres, cross at the lights towards Georgian St Botolph's, Aldersgate, a church that did survive the Great Fire, but was subsequently rebuilt in the late eighteenth century. Just to the left of the church is the entrance to Postman's Park, marked by a towering **London Plane** and an elegant 'Atropurpurea' cultivar of **Japanese Maple**.

Entrance to the Park requires negotiating steps: for those who may find this challenging, skip the Park by turning down Little Britain to the north of the church and then left on King Edward Street to the park's western gate. The park, a sliver of green between the two main roads, has two principal attractions. The first is the Memorial to Heroic Self-Sacrifice, while the other is a glorious **Handkerchief Tree**. These plants

Handkerchief Tree

come into their own during early May when they produce copious and exuberant blooms resembling linen handkerchiefs hanging from the branches. Outside its flowering time, it is easy to miss, a slightly gangly medium-sized tree towards the southern wall just beyond the memorial.

Beyond the Handkerchief Tree, you will see a **Whitebeam**, the seemingly inevitable **Tree Ferns** – a staple of City parklets – and more planes, before you leave the park via the exit onto King Edward Street where you turn left. Look down Angel Street on your left to admire a recently planted row of fastigiate **'Dawyck' Beeches**, before crossing and making for the corner of King Edward Street and Newgate Street. Here, another blitzed Wren church, Christ Church Greyfriars, has been turned into a treeless – but colourfully floral – garden with the extant tower at its western end.

Cross at the lights, with an **American Sweetgum** to your right and another on the south side of the crossing. Follow Newgate Street round to the left as it turns back towards St Paul's: the station entrance is on the left after about 70 metres.

Postman's Park

Postman's Park is so-called because of its position adjacent to the site of the General Post Office, a grand classical building demolished in 1912. The Park's intriguing story is emblematic of the City of London.

It is large by City standards, but minuscule on most other measures. Its footprint is an irregular shape caused by its nineteenth-century amalgamation of no fewer than three former burial grounds. St Botolph's Aldersgate is the eastern portion, next to its church, while the western parcel belonged to Christ Church Greyfriars (destroyed in the Blitz), and a small square in the south-east was that of St Leonard, Foster Lane (a church not rebuilt after the Great Fire).

Entrance to Postman's Park on St Martin's Le Grand

By the early 1800s, the City's ancient churchyards were so full of burials that bodies were placed on top of older graves, and increasingly unsanitary conditions eventually led to the banning of new internments. The ground in some churchyards had been raised by the actions of stacking, as was the case in St Botolph's, where the ground was reportedly 6 feet above that of Christ Church Greyfriars. Undulations in the ground are still discernible, corresponding to the various burial jurisdictions, and also account for the steps into the Park from St Martin's Le Grand.

As well as the magnificent Handkerchief Tree, Postman's Park is home, like many corners of the City, to several monuments erected down the centuries to remember people, events or institutions. One of the most celebrated is its Memorial to Heroic Self-Sacrifice, a wooden loggia housing ceramic plaques. This peculiarly quaint, yet morbid installation is the work of a now obscure Victorian artist, G. F. Watts, whose paintings of symbolically charged and romantic subjects were hugely popular in their day. The ornate ceramic plaques remember individual acts of tragic self-immolation on a Hardyesque scale. Typical among them is:

William Donald of Bayswater. Aged 19. Railway Clerk. Was drowned in the Lea trying to save a lad from a dangerous entanglement of weed. July 16 1876

Plane avenue , Inner Temple Gardens

Legal London

Holborn to Temple

This short walk from Holborn to Temple guides you through the heart of legal London by way its fascinating rare and aged trees. Starting in Edwardian Holborn next to one of London's busiest junctions, you will amble through some surprisingly tranquil corners of the borderland between the City and the West End. Highlights include London's largest square, one of London's loveliest, some of its least-visited gardens, and buildings even older than the trees.

Length: 2 miles (4,000 steps)
Start: Holborn Tube station (Central and Piccadilly Lines)
Finish: Temple Tube station (District and Circle Lines)
Accessibility: Pavements and level surfaces, crossing some busy roads, unavoidable steps and some unmade paths
Relative Difficulty: 2/5

1 – Holborn Tube station to the Strand

Turn left on Kingsway as you leave Holborn Station. This grand Edwardian avenue opened in 1905 to connect the Strand with High Holborn, sweeping away a maze of slums and interconnecting streets in its path.

Although Kingsway is particularly wide, and was built during the height of London's street-tree-planting boom (between 1870 and 1914), the trees seen today were not planted until 1947. In the intervening decades the trees, mostly **London Planes** and a couple of Trees of Heaven, have matured, albeit with a distinct lean away from the buildings, and look as if they have always been here.

After just a few metres, turn left on narrow Gate Street, passing the alley of New Turnstile and, next to the Ship Inn, Little Turnstile, where the road curves right and opens up to reveal the canopy of Lincoln's Inn Fields ahead. You should ignore the entrance to the square immediately opposite the end of Gate Street, and turn left along its

north side. About a third of the way along, stop to admire Sir John Soane's Museum. This is the former home, now an excellent and free museum, of the architect of Pitshanger Manor (featured in our exploration of Ealing, see page 168), along with many other notable early nineteenth-century buildings.

Continue straight on past the next entrance to the Fields until you reach the north-east corner and Newman's Row, where you may like to take a moment to admire the **London Planes** hanging over the old wall. They are the rare and intriguing **'Baobab'** variety. Now enter the square, through the gate next to Barry Flanagan's sheet metal 'Camdonian' sculpture of 1980. Turn right to follow the path west along

Lincoln's Inn Fields bandstand

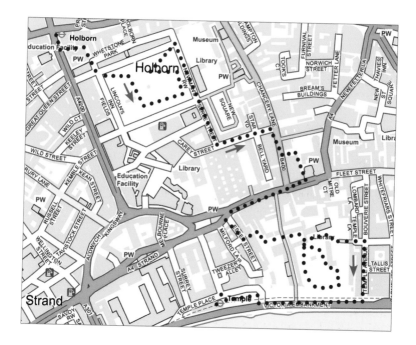

the northern edge, with several stops until you draw level with the entrance gate just before the Soane's museum. The first tree you'll see is a fenced-in **Sugar Maple**, a memorial tree planted by the former Canadian Prime Minister Jean Chrétien. It is the species from which the Canadian maple leaf symbol is derived, and the source of maple syrup. A little further along, a fine **Judas Tree** is set against the fence, followed by a pair of **Southern Catalpas** either side of the gate.

From here, turn left, making for the wooden pavilion at the centre of the Fields, passing a blowsy, pink-flowering **'Kanzan' Cherry** on your right. The paved central area is encircled by venerable planes, but you must turn left to see some of the Fields' stoutest, and probably oldest, **London**

Aged London Plane

Magnolia will be laden with large white blooms. This tree has a plaque at its base, revealing it was planted in 1953. Just beyond are a pair of **Persian Ironwoods**, that come into their own in the autumn with fine leaf colouring, a kaleidoscopic mix of orange and scarlet through to deep purple.

Leave the Fields by the gate in the south-east corner, to be faced with the looming Victorian Gothic structures of Lincoln's Inn, one of the four Inns of Court. Despite the 'Private, No Thoroughfare' sign on the gatehouse, it is usually possible to enter this legal sanctuary, where there is a lot to admire both architecturally and arboreally. This walk steels itself for the legal-arboreal prizes of the Temple, however, but a peek through Lincoln's Inn gate to admire the towering **London Planes** is recommended.

From Lincoln's Inn Fields, turn right and continue south down Serle Street towards yet more Gothic invention, in the shape of the Royal Courts of Justice, pausing to note the Ginkgos on Portugal Street. As you approach the courts – a vast Victorian mediaeval fantasy on a par with St Pancras Station or J. K. Rowling's Hogwarts – turn left into Carey Street, lined on its southern side with **Dawn Redwoods**.

These fine examples have been here for barely 30 years, but already they are huge and add great distinction to the court buildings. A recommended stop here, the Seven Stars pub, offers a fine vantage point from which to admire the symphony of stone, plant and, oddly, red phone box.

At the end of Carey Street, turn right on treeless Chancery Lane, with more Gothic finery, King's College London's Maughan

Lincoln's Inn Fields' subtropical garden

Planes. As you approach the eastern gate, you pass through a dense belt of subtropical planting on your right, which you can walk through to discover exotic species including a **Mimosa**, a **Persian Silk Tree**, **Chusan Palms**, a **Loquat** and a **Canary Palm**.

Beyond this luxuriant grove, turn right, keeping the perimeter to your left. If you are visiting in March, an exceptional **Kobushi**

Lincoln's Inn Fields

London's largest square, Lincoln's Inn Fields is also – nearly – its oldest, having been laid out in the 1630s (only Covent Garden is older, but it's a rather different beast these days).

Unlike many of London's other squares, Lincoln's Inn was not conceived as a garden square, nor as a single architectural statement with consistent terraces around its perimeter.

Instead, the Fields were originally open land next to Lincoln's Inn on the edge of the City. This era is recalled in some of the street names: Gate Street, Little, New and Great Turnstiles remind us not that Lincoln's Inn Fields was an exclusive, gated address, but that it was used to graze livestock, with these obstacles to discourage them from wandering off into the West End. During the seventeenth century it became a fashionable address for wealthy Londoners, and several buildings from this era survive including the oldest, Lindsey House at 59-60.

During the eighteenth century it had become popular with lawyers attracted by its proximity to the Inns of Court. Other professions followed: in 1792 the architect Sir John Soane moved in to number 12, and over the next four decades redeveloped it and neighbouring properties at numbers 13 and 14 as his home, office and then his museum, which has been here ever since his death in 1837.

It could be said that London's largest residential square came about unintentionally, but the appeal of squares was not lost on subsequent planners and architects, who modelled much of the city's Georgian

Sir John Soane's Museum

development on the formula of grand housing around a communal, but usually private, garden square.

By 1735 the Fields were laid out with a formal scheme of grass with gravel walks, and over the subsequent decades it seems likely that some of what are now the largest plane trees were planted. The gardens came into official public ownership in 1894, and have been continually maintained and developed since then.

Middle and Inner Temple

Middle Temple Hall in the seventeenth century

The Temple, consisting of the Middle and Inner Temples, but no Outer, represents two of the Inns of Court, the heart of London's (and England and Wales's) legal profession. The others are Lincoln's Inn and, a little further away, Gray's Inn.

They act as professional, training and regulatory bodies for barristers, who must be a member of one of the Inns.

The Temple's name is derived from the Knights Templar, the military-monastic order who occupied the site until they were suppressed in 1312, but not before they had built the Temple Church with its round nave, a feature peculiar to Templar ecclesiastical design. Following their suppression, the Temple started being let to legal practitioners, while passing into the ownership of the Knights Hospitaller. By this time the Temple was split into two parts: unconsecrated Middle and consecrated Inner Temples.

Following the Reformation, the Temple reverted to the Crown, and eventually the barristers themselves. Since then it has evolved slowly into the cloistered legal sanctuary it is today. Each of the Inns of Court has its own institutions, including a great hall, a library, administration buildings, chambers (from where the barristers practice), enclosed gardens and a chapel, although Inner and Middle Temple share the Temple Church.

Until the 1870s, both the Middle and Inner Temple Gardens were considerably smaller, and fronted directly onto the river, but the construction of the Embankment saw a large amount of land reclaimed and added as southern extensions.

Library, on your left. Immediately after the library, turn left on a gated alley leading past some impressively topiaried **Yew** pyramids. You are now within the City of London. The passage abruptly turns right just past a **False Acacia**, and emerges as Clifford's Inn Passage via a gatehouse onto Fleet Street. The gatehouse is all that survives of Clifford's Inn, a former Inn of Chancery that closed in 1903 and was demolished in 1934.

Turn right on Fleet Street, passing the half-timbered Inner Temple Gateway on the south side of the street, and cross Chancery Lane and Bell Yard until you reach the front expanse of the Royal Courts. Note the ornately mounted dragon of Temple Bar in the middle of the road marking the boundary of the City of London, and where Fleet Street becomes the Strand.

Cross over the Strand via the zebra crossing and turn into a discreet passage, Devereux Court, to the left of the faux-timbered George pub. To your right, the Strand splits around the plane tree-lined island of St Clement Danes church, the Central Church of the RAF, which was largely rebuilt after being pretty much gutted by fire during the war. The two statues outside it are of Hugh Dowding, who commanded Fighter Command during the Battle of Britain, and the altogether more controversial figure of Arthur Harris, who dedicated Bomber Command so determinedly to the area bombing of German cities.

Follow the alley around a couple of right angles before you see a black door amid white stucco and ironwork on your left. An antique sign points to 'New Court, Temple' beyond.

Dawn Redwood on Carey Street

2 – Middle Temple to Temple Tube station

Temple Church

loveliest, particularly in late July and August when they are covered in ripe fruits.

From the fountain, turn left past the old **London Planes** and the fabulous sixteenth-century Middle Temple Hall, said to be central London's finest Elizabethan building. Just before the Hall you can admire the Middle Temple Garden, a long green strip that is worth a detour if you have the time. This walk, however, holds out for the Inner Temple Garden.

Fountain Court opens onto Middle Temple Lane, a gently sloping stone-flagged thoroughfare leading from Fleet Street to the Embankment that is the boundary between the Middle and Inner Temples. Turn left briefly, before ducking through a stone archway into Pump Court, and the Inner Temple, on your right. It is a somewhat gloomy court enlivened by a pair of evergreen **Tree Cotoneasters**. At the far side, head under the vaulted arcade to emerge into Church Court, with Temple Church on your left.

Apart from a few youngish planes, there is little to distract you from admiring this remarkable church. The circular nave dates from the twelfth century, while the rest is from the thirteenth century (with some restoration in subsequent centuries). Next to the church, an immaculately clipped **Hornbeam** hedge hides the handsome Master's House and its small garden refuge, a post-war reconstruction of a 1667 building.

Pass through another stone-clad portal, this time a simpler rectangular affair, to arrive in King's Bench Walk, a

Crossing the threshold of Little Gate from Devereux Court into the Middle Temple is to enter another world. It is a peaceful and attractive place, akin to a vast Oxbridge college, exuding wealth, privilege and ancient traditions.

You have arrived in New Court, from where you turn right down the short flight of steps into Fountain Court, towards a **Chinese Tree Privet** directly in front of you and the round fountain beyond it. The fountain is London's first, dating from 1681, but the most remarkable thing about Fountain Court is the pair of twisted and ancient-looking **Black Mulberries** arching over it.

Despite their aged appearance, they are considerably younger than the fountain, having been planted for Queen Victoria's Golden Jubilee in 1887. These remarkable trees are just two of the arboreal treasures the Temple has to offer, but are among the

Inner Temple Gardens

The Inner Temple Gardens are some of the finest and least visited in London. They are beautifully kept by a team of gardeners who tend to the magnificent shrubberies, herbaceous borders, lawns and, of course, the trees, many of which are labelled.

There are lots of noteworthy trees to admire. Here is a clockwise tour of some highlights that caught the author's eye, starting and finishing from the Crown Office Row gate, itself a splendid piece of eighteenth- century ironwork. As you descend the steps, a **Hybrid Strawberry Tree** on the left is a taste of what lies ahead.

Next is a bluey-grey-foliaged **'Glauca' Atlas Cedar,** followed by a low, spreading tree, a rare **Manchurian Walnut.** Follow Paper Buildings round to the left beyond a young **Cucumber Tree**, a **Japanese Zelkova** and a very plump and elderly **Sargent's Cherry,** to where a green alcove hides another characterful **Black Mulberry**.

Hybrid Strawberry Tree

A little way out from the perimeter, look out for a recently planted horticultural oddity: a **Phoenix Snakebark Maple**. It is a multi-stemmed tree with rather sickly-looking leaves, but very conspicuous veined creamy white and green bark. You will, no doubt, have already noticed the **Dawn Redwood** that dominates the eastern edge of the garden. It is not as tall as the trees on Carey Street but, judging by its stouter trunk, appears to be somewhat older.

At the southern end of the gardens lies an impressive array of **London Planes**. There are three huge trees, consisting of a single specimen and a pair, which together are thought to date from the 1770s, and

beyond is a whole avenue of planes forming the boundary with the Embankment. The avenue is formed of rows that were clearly planted at different times: the northern row is older – nineteenth century – while the southern row might date from the early twentieth century.

At the western end of the plane avenue is something of the red corner: look out for **Paul's Scarlet Hawthorns**, a **Scarlet Oak** and a **Red Maple** before making your way back up the perimeter past a young **Tupelo** towards a stately **Tulip Tree**. Finally, delve into the far corner to locate a rare **Catalina Ironwood**, before following the fence round to the gate on Crown Office Row.

Black Mulberry

Morus nigra

Humans have had a long relationship with the alluring, fruit-bearing Black Mulberry tree. Its precise native range is unclear, muddled by its association with migrating and trading people over millennia, but western Asia seems likely.

Developing Mulberries

According to English mythology, the species arrived on our shores in the early 1600s, sponsored by royalty.

Many will have heard about James I's introduction of mulberries in the hope of kickstarting an English silk industry. Unfortunately, so the story goes, he imported the wrong species – silkworms feed on the leaves of White rather than Black Mulberries – and James's seventeenth-century industrial diversification plan failed, but arboreal remnants of this royal initiative can still be seen in quiet corners all over London.

The story is partly true: James did import the wrong species for silkworm fodder, but he was not the one who introduced it. Archaeologists have discovered Roman-era mulberry seeds in the City, and it seems likely that fresh mulberries have been on the menu at religious houses, aristocratic manors and educational institutions since well before James transported shiploads of saplings from the continent.

Mulberry trees – as the Temple duo prove – age attractively, taking on a characterfully gnarled and tortured appearance suggesting great age. There are dozens of similarly distinctive trees dotted around, many with stories stretching back centuries, and some claiming to have been part of James's original stock. But the Temple trees are a mere 150 years old, most definitely not relics of the ill-fated Jacobean silk industry, and remind us that dating living trees is an imprecise science.

Black Mulberry trees may not produce leaves to the liking of silkworms, but they do produce considerably better fruit. White mulberries are rather dry and tasteless compared to the sweet and juicy fruits borne by Black Mulberries. These delicious fruits have always attracted those in the know, but their physical delicacy leads to easy bruising, causing their deep red juice to ooze over the hands of mulberry gatherers. A word of caution – seek permission before helping yourself in the Temple to avoid being caught red-handed.

wide, paved expanse surrounded by tall terraced chambers set with some splendid straight-trunked **London Planes**. The illusion of having stepped back in time is shattered here by the rows of expensive cars that clog the place. Turn right briefly on King's Bench Walk, before turning right again into Crown Office Row with the stone-clad Paper Buildings on your left, and just beyond the expanse of Inner Temple Gardens.

As the road curves slightly, make for the gate in the fence midway along where you can enter the gardens. Note that the gardens are only open between 12.30 and 3.00 on weekdays; at other times Crown Office Row is not a bad grandstand from which to admire the magnificent trees within.

From the gardens, head back onto King's Bench Walk and a gap between the buildings marked by an **American Sweetgum** and a **Purple Cherry Plum**, which spits you out of the Temple and the reverie it has no doubt induced, into the relatively real world of the City of London. You are now on Tudor Street, and after a few metres turn right on Temple Avenue leading to Victoria Embankment.

Turn right on the Embankment, admiring the Inner Temple Gardens' plane avenue from a different perspective. At one time, the gardens fronted straight onto the river, which would have been a much wider channel before the construction of the Embankment between 1865 and 1870 (see more on the following pages). Indeed, the northern row of trees in the gardens' avenue may well date from that time, and marks roughly where the river would once have lapped.

Walk past the gates to Middle Temple Lane, noting the emblems of the Inner Temple (a pegasus on blue ground) on the right-hand gate, and the lamb and flag of Middle Temple on the subsequent three gates. Beyond them is another chance to peek into Middle Temple Garden.

Cross Temple Place and enter the Temple Section of Victoria Embankment Gardens, the first of a string of ornamental gardens lining the northern side of the Embankment laid out on land reclaimed from the Thames. This small garden is stuffed with trees; most are unremarkable, but in the middle, occupying a grass oval, are a pair of blue-flowering **Foxglove Trees**. At the trees, take the slight right fork to leave the gardens in the north-west corner. From here, the entrance to Temple Tube station is down the steps to your left.

City boundary on the Embankment

London Planes line Victoria Embankment

The Embankment's
Nineteenth-Century Planes

Temple to Westminster

The final walk in this book is a chance to appreciate
London's crowning arboreal glory: the London Plane. It is a
short route, following a curve of the River Thames, tracing
one of London's earliest and most conspicuous tree-lined
thoroughfares. We look at the grand riverside buildings and
the ornamental gardens along the way.
While it is a route defined by London Planes, there are
plenty of other trees to admire.

Length: 1 mile (2,000 steps)
Start: Temple Station (District and Circle Lines)
Finish: Westminster Station (District, Circle and Jubilee Lines)
Accessibility: Pavements and level surfaces, crossing some busy roads,
unavoidable steps.
Relative Difficulty: 1/5

1 – Temple Tube station to Embankment Tube station

With the entrance to Temple Station behind you, turn left and then almost immediately go up the steps onto the asphalt station roof and riverside vantage point.

This barren terrace is nothing to write home about: there is no shelter or catering – an overlooked opportunity, perhaps.

But what it does offer is a chance to get up close and personal with a mature **London Plane** canopy, something all too difficult when most trees have been trained to allow the unhindered passage of a high-sided van or lorry underneath. In spring, just as the trees are bursting into leaf, it is an opportunity to witness close-up the unfolding of the trees' iconic, and briefly delicate, leaves from their winter dormancy.

This is the time that planes come into flower too. Their distinctive seedballs, that hang in clusters of twos or occasionally threes, are preceded by very similar flowers. Trees bear both male and female flowers, which look fairly similar, but the female flowers tend to be larger and, fleetingly, have a red dusting of inflorescences.

As well as a springtime viewing plat-form for London plane flowers, the Temple roof also allows you to comprehend this walk's entire route, and the nineteenth-century engineering marvel of the Victoria Embankment, that stretches from Blackfriars Bridge in the east to Westminster and the Houses of Parliament in the west. It appears to be an almost unbroken avenue of **London Planes**, but behind the busy road lies a chain of delightful gardens where many other trees can be found.

Go down the steps at the western end of the Temple terrace where, opposite a row of **Ginkgos** on Temple Place, a green cabman's shelter offers reasonably priced takeaway drinks, snacks and hot food on the bacon sarnie trajectory. There are thirteen of these traditional wooden huts scattered across central London catering to taxi drivers (and others).

Sixty-one were built between 1875 and 1914, offering sustenance and shelter for cabbies in what was essentially a move to stop drivers drinking on the job by offering an alternative to the pub. Funded by well-meaning and inevitably puritanical Victorians, gambling, the shelters were stocked with improving publications, and drinking and swearing were strictly prohibited.

Just beyond the terrace, the smallest of the Embankment Gardens is on your left. A scrappy mix of **False Acacias**, **Cherry Plums** and **Holm Oaks**, it is chiefly of interest for the monument to Isambard Kingdom

London Plane flowers

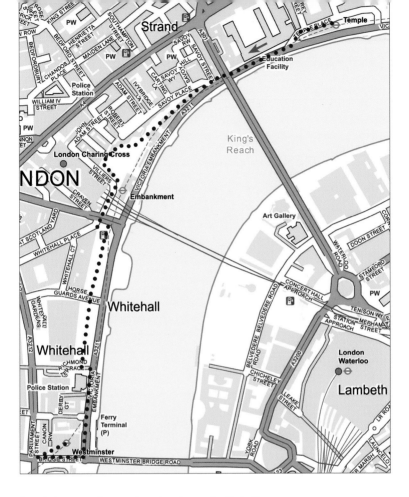

Brunel, the great railway engineer (see the Docklands walk on page 70 for one of his achievements), at the corner where Temple Place joins Victoria Embankment.

Brunel died in 1859, more than a decade before the Victoria Embankment was opened. His statue is placed here simply because it is a prominent spot, rather than to commemorate any involvement in the construction of the Embankment, although Brunel was a champion of its engineer, Joseph Bazalgette. So perhaps it is a kind of homage.

Past the statue, cross over Victoria Embankment and continue along with the river on your left and the great ramparts of Somerset House across the road on your right. The trees on either side of the street here are exclusively **London Planes**, the species originally selected to line this route. Whether these individual trees are original is debatable; some may well be, but many are certainly replacements. They are clearly smaller and less thriving than some you will

The Victoria Embankment

York Watergate in Victoria Embankment Gardens demonstrates just how much wider the river was before the Thames was embanked. In its broad, pre-embanked days, the river meandered at a much more stately pace, lapping at waterside gardens and piers from Chelsea to the Temple.

The National Liberal Club, 1890s

By the mid-nineteenth century, the state of London's river frontage had become something of an embarrassment, and in 1858 the 'Great Stink', when raw sewage on the shoreline combined with hot weather, forced the government to act. The civil engineer Joseph Bazalgette was engaged to construct 82 miles of sewers to take London's domestic and industrial waste away from the city. Part of this mammoth task was the construction of main sewers on either side of the river, enclosed within new embankments: the Victoria, Chelsea and Albert Embankments.

The first to be built was the Victoria Embankment, which was begun in 1864 and completed in 1870, with the gardens following in 1874. Trees started appearing in 1869, to the relief of many who had been advocating the construction of Parisian-style tree-lined boulevards for decades. Indeed, before the Victoria Embankment was constructed and trees were planted along its length, the only other example in London was Margaretta Terrace and its adjoining streets, laid out by John Samuel Phené in 1851 (see page 165).

It is impossible to overstate the revolutionary impact the Victoria Embankment had on London. Not only did it reclaim a ribbon of land which at its widest point is well over 100 metres, it also improved the environment, both through the sewers encased within it and by systematically planting trees and laying out public gardens along its length. But perhaps the Embankment's greatest legacy is the choice of tree species: the hybrid London Plane, planted along it so conspicuously and proving so successful as a city tree.

encounter in the gardens along this route, but the privations of their frontline position mean their growth will undoubtedly be hindered. If some of these trees are 150 years old, it is perhaps even more remarkable.

As you pass under Waterloo Bridge, Victoria Embankment Gardens appears on the right. Cross back over to enter the gardens on the corner of Savoy Place, with a particularly grand London Plane behind you at the foot of Waterloo Bridge. Relief from the thundering traffic is immediate as you enter the wedge-shaped gardens past several **Persian Ironwoods**.

The gardens gradually open out past more planting, including **Ornamental Cherries**, a **Juneberry** or two, a **Mimosa** and a **Père David's Maple**, one of the snakebark maples which are so difficult to tell apart. Père David's is the most frequent of them, its unusual name derived from the French missionary Father Armand David who, in between his colonial missionary work, travelled extensively in China, sending back to France news and samples of exciting botanical and zoological 'discoveries'. As well as his eponymous maple, David is remembered in the botanical name of the handkerchief tree, *Davidia involucrata*, and for Père David's deer.

After 50 metres or so, past more **Persian Ironwoods** and the first of the garden's Planes, you will also encounter the first of its statues, a high camp memorial consisting of a bronze bust raised on a stone plinth around which an inconsolable semi-naked woman is draped. This is Arthur Sullivan, one half of Victorian light operatic duo Gilbert and Sullivan, whose works were for many years performed at the Savoy Theatre within the famous hotel just above. As well as a delightful oasis with dozens of interesting trees, the Embankment Gardens complex serves as one of London's most densely populated Victorian and Edwardian monumental sculpture parks.

Beyond an entrance to the Savoy Hotel flanked by a pair of **Chinese Tree Privets** on the right, the gardens start to widen, and some larger trees will catch your attention. The first is a **Dawn Redwood**, complete with a plaque telling us that it was planted in 1971 and, underneath its botanical name, providing a common name of 'Fossil Tree'. Now out of use, this sobriquet is testament to how plant names evolve.

A little further along is a stout **Southern Catalpa**, with a plaque stating it was planted for Queen Elizabeth's coronation in 1953. Both this and the Dawn Redwood show how

Chinese Tree Privet

London Plane

Platanus x hispanica

No London tree book could be complete without mention of the species that defines this city more than any other: the London Plane.

London is not the natural home of London Planes. They are a hybrid, the result of the intermingling of two related species from different corners of the world: the Oriental Plane from south-east Europe and western Asia, and the American Sycamore from eastern North America. Various myths have been created about the hybrid plane's origin. One says that the hybridisation occurred in Oxford, another that it was in Lambeth, but Spain or France are more realistic. Regardless of where the hybridisation occurred, the salient point is that they are a product of human actions. It was us that brought the parent species together, and caused a union that would never have happened in nature.

London Planes are therefore not 'native' to specific regions, but they do thrive in cities, so it could be said they are the world's

first urban tree. They arrived here around 1680, and for decades were occasional curiosities known as the hybrid or bastard plane tree. Things started to change in the eighteenth century. when planes were selected for some of London's new squares and public spaces. There are trees in Lincoln's Inn Fields and Inner Temple Garden, St Paul's Churchyard and Cheapside that date from the 1700s.

It was not until the nineteenth century that their popularity really took off here, and even then there was at least one false start. Following the example of Paris and other European cities, they had been planted on the streets of Chelsea in 1850 (see page 163), but it was not until they were planted on the new Victoria Embankment in 1870 that people really took notice of these attractive and pollution-tolerant trees.

rapidly trees can grow, as well as reminding us of how their names are subject to change. Southern Catalpa seems like a much more appropriate name for a tree otherwise popularly known as an Indian Bean Tree, named not for the subcontinent but for Native Americans, this being a tree originating from the southern US.

As the gardens broaden, and more monuments mingle with the trees, look out for some **Honey Locusts** on your right just before you arrive by the first of the grand and broad planes, this one a burry **'Pyramidalis'** type, its growth unhindered by pollarding.

Beyond, a rather unhealthy-looking young tree can be seen on the left: a **Wollemi Pine**, the contemporary 'living fossil' tree. Like the Dawn Redwood (see page 91), Wollemi Pines were known from the Southern Hemisphere fossil record and in 1994, remarkably, a living population was discovered 100 miles from Sydney. Since then, the tree has been propagated widely, and examples can be found in many corners of the world.

As you pass the enchanting miniature statue featuring a pith-helmeted soldier on a camel – the memorial to the Imperial Camel Corps – the **London Plane** canopy gives way to open lawns and a choice of paths. Take the right fork to hug the northern boundary, edged by more planes. The last of these is particularly noteworthy, with a rather more ungainly stature to the others: it appears to be closer to an **Oriental Plane** than a London Plane. The problem with planes is there are many different cultivars, many of which are unrecorded, and some are quite borderline between being a hybrid London Plane or a true Oriental Plane.

The last stop in the gardens is, next to a magnificent **Tree of Heaven**, York Watergate from 1626. When constructed, its steps led directly into the Thames, enabling the residents of palatial York House, one of many grand abodes that once lined the river, to step into a waiting boat to be whisked along London's great connecting artery.

From here turn left past the Open-Air Theatre, and then right on a path leading you out past a nondescript brick building – Charing Cross Substation – to emerge outside Embankment Tube station, with Villiers Street on your right and Embankment Place straight ahead under Hungerford Bridge, which carries the railway into Charing Cross Station.

York Watergate and Tree of Heaven

2 – Northumberland Avenue to Westminster

Having passed through Embankment Place, you emerge on Northumberland Avenue, a street constructed in 1876 to connect the new Victoria Embankment with the older streets converging at Charing Cross. In keeping with the grand tree-lined thoroughfare at its southern end, this was designed to be planted with **London Planes**. At considerable expense, pits for the trees were constructed. A contemporary report by Clerk of the Improvements Committee, Percy J. Edwards, explains:

To secure the well-being of trees, pits were formed and filled with proper soil, and the footway surrounding the trees was covered with an open grating to admit the rain and air to the soil, and to enable it to be stirred and kept loose on the surface. The grating and footway were supported independently by girders over the pits, so as to prevent the settlement of the paving and the hardening of the ground around the roots of the trees.

Having admired the planes – possibly not the originals, judging by their relatively meagre size – which lean away from the ornate architecture of a street built to impress, it is worth ascending the pedestrian Golden Jubilee Bridge to get an elevated view of the Embankment west to the Palace of Westminster. It is a particularly instructive view in winter, when the planes are not in leaf and you can see more clearly the splendour of the National Liberal Club behind the first section of Whitehall Gardens, our next destination.

Once back at street level, cross Victoria Embankment at the lights and turn right to inspect the memorial to Joseph Bazalgette on the river. Just past the first London Plane beyond the memorial (a relatively young specimen), cross back at the next set of lights to enter Whitehall Gardens by the south-eastern gate.

Unlike Victoria Embankment Gardens, the first section of Whitehall Gardens has a regular rectangular shape laid out in a formal scheme around three statues of Victorian eminences, each contained within its own circular lawn resplendent with **Cabbage Palms**, and each lawn utilising a different cultivar with contrasting leaf colours. The gardens are edged with soaring **London Planes**, but other species are hiding within . . .

Cabbage Palms

Recumbent Southern Catalpa

Take the path along the northern fringe, from where you can admire the gardens' preeminent arboreal treasures: a series of aged **Southern Catalpas** in various stages of prostration. This species lives fast and dies young. If these were oaks, a casual admirer might expect them to be centuries old, but they are only as old as the reclaimed land on which they are planted, so a maximum of a century and a half. The most enigmatic of the bunch is nearly horizontal, held aloft by a series of steel props, and is a favourite climbing tree for children allowed to engage in such risky activities.

Elsewhere, the lawns support small green weeping trees in each corner – **Weeping White Mulberries** – which in years to come could develop as much craggy allure as the Catalpas. Among the understorey trees helping to screen the road to the south and to frame the National Liberal Club on its northern edge, these gardens host a broad selection of trees including a culinary trio of **Fig**, **Olive** and **Bay**.

Leave the first section of Whitehall Gardens by a flight of four steps, marked by a white-veined **Snakebark Maple**, onto Horse Guards Avenue, or, if you would rather avoid the steps, by a gate onto the main Victoria Embankment road, and head round the corner.

Some of the finest planes on the whole stretch of the Embankment are those around this junction. At least one is unequivocally an **Oriental Plane**, which might be identified by its incised leaves, together with small seed balls and flowers held in bunches of up to seven. A London plane will have larger flowers, and fruits typically held in twos or threes.

Cross Horse Guards Avenue to enter the final section of Whitehall Gardens, which is again rather different in character from its preceding garden and the Victoria

The Street Tree Craze

Guiseppe De Nittis, The Victoria Embankment, London, 1875

As we have seen in Chelsea with the example of Margaretta Terrace, planting trees on London's streets got off to a slow start. It was not until the opening of the Victoria Embankment in 1870 that London really started to embrace this new, continental idea.

London's love affair with the hybrid plane started on the Embankment, and became an emblem of the modern city. But the inspiration for the tree-lined avenue came from European cities like Paris and Berlin. Hausmann's redevelopment of Paris in the mid-nineteenth century introduced broad, plane-tree-lined 'grands boulevards' into contemporary city planning.

So London was actually late to the party – indeed, before the late-nineteenth-century urban trees were confined to the city's squares, and walks: tree-lined promenades in places such as Kensington Gardens and St James's Park.

Following the success of the Embankment, it became a model for London's own grand, tree-lined thoroughfares. During the decades between the development of the Embankment and the First World War, planes were planted at an eye-watering rate. By 1920, one commentator, A. D. Webster, was able to say that 60% of London's street trees were planes.

Civic leaders from around the country and beyond wanted to emulate London's new-found arboreal grandeur, and so a plane-tree-planting craze started, and streets around the country, not to mention the rest of the English-speaking world, were, for the next 40 years, planted with planes. It was during this period as thousands were planted from Acton to Walthamstow, and from Brooklyn to Melbourne, that they acquired the name 'London Plane', in reference to their transformation of the capital.

Embankment Gardens too. It is more open, and its right-hand edge is not tree-lined, so the Portland stone edifice of the Ministry of Defence dominates. The garden is stuffed with military monuments, along with one or two **Southern Catalpas** and a handful of **Oriental Planes**, but otherwise it is exclusively populated with **London Planes**.

Pass through this garden to exit at the corner of Richmond Road and Victoria Embankment. Continue along the plane-lined pavement, passing New Scotland Yard on your right, with the Houses of Parliament and the Elizabeth clock tower, housing Big Ben, straight ahead.

Continue past Portcullis House and cross Bridge Street until you are directly underneath the Elizabeth Tower and Big Ben, clad in scaffolding and hoardings at the time of writing. Immediately to the right of the tower is New Palace Yard which, although closed to the public, is visible through the

substantial railings. At its centre is a lawn surrounded by pleached limes, probably **Common Limes**, a style once much favoured for formal gardens, and now relatively rare. But the most remarkable trees here are the **Southern Catalpas** that line the wall. These heavily pollarded Victorian trees could be even older than those in Whitehall Gardens.

The Victorians were clearly fond of Catalpas: no doubt the combination of large, fragrant leaves, conspicuous summer flowers and curious bean-like seed pods contrived to make them a must-have tree for new civic plantings. They are a tree which has been in and out of fashion over the decades, but, being large, spreading trees, they appear to be rather out of fashion these days.

From the crossing at the corner of Bridge Street and Parliament Square, cross back over to enter Westminster Tube station on the corner of Parliament Street.

Wizened Southern Catalpa in New Palace Yard

Species List

List of tree and shrub species mentioned in the book in alphabetical order by common name

Alder, European	*Alnus glutinosa*
Alder, Italian	*Alnus cordata*
Alder, Spaeth's	*Alnus x spaethii*
Almond	*Prunus dulcis*
Ash	*Fraxinus excelsior*
Weeping	*'Pendula'*
One-leaved	*'Diversifolia'*
Ash, Green	*Fraxinus pennsylvanica*
Ash, Manna	*Fraxinus ornus*
Ash, Narrow-leaved	*Fraxinus angustifolia*
Raywood	*'Raywood'*
Weeping	*'Pendula'*
Aspen	*Populus tremula*
Bay	*Laurus nobilis*
Bee-bee Tree	*Tetradium daniellii*
Beech	*Fagus sylvatica*
Copper	*'Purpurea'*
	'Dawyck'
Birch, Chinese Red	*Betula albosinensis*
Birch, Downy	*Betula pubescens*
Birch, Erman's	*Betula ermanii*
Birch, Himalayan	*Betula utilis var. jacquemontii*
Birch, River	*Betula nigra*
Birch, Silver	*Betula pendula*
Weeping	*'Youngii'*
Blackthorn	*Prunus spinosa*
Blackwood	*Acacia melanoxylon*
Bottlebrush Tree	*Callistemon citrinus*
Bramble	*Rubus fruticosus*
Catalpa, Southern	*Catalpa bignonioides*
Golden	*'Aurea'*
	'Nana'
Cedar of Lebanon	*Cedrus libani*
Cedar, Atlas	*Cedrus atlantica*
	'Glauca'
Cedar, Deodar	*Cedrus deodara*
Cherry Plum	*Prunus cerasifera*
Purple	*'Nigra'*
Purple	*'Pissardii'*
Cherry, Bird	*Prunus padus*

Cherry, Manchurian	*Prunus maackii*
	'Amber Beauty'
Cherry, Ornamental	*Prunus serrulata*
	'Snow Goose'
	'Umineko'
	'Kanzan'
	'Shirotae'
	'Accolade'
Cherry, Sargent's	*Prunus sargentii*
Cherry, Tibetan	*Prunus serrula*
Cherry, Wild or Gean	*Prunus avium*
	'Plena'
Cherry, Winter-flowering	*Prunus x subhirtella*
	'Autumnalis'
Cotoneaster, Tree	*Cotoneaster frigidus*
Crabapple, Chonosuki	*Malus tschonoskii*
Crabapple, Erect	*Eriolobus trilobatus*
Cucumber Tree	*Magnolia acuminata*
Cypress, Italian	*Cupressus sempervirens*
Cypress, Lawson's	*Chamaecyparis lawsoniana*
Cypress, Leyland	*x Cupressocyparis leylandii*
Cypress, Monterey	*Cupressus macrocarpa*
Cypress, Nootka	*Xanthocyparis nootkatensis*
Cypress, Swamp	*Taxodium distichum*
Elder	*Sambucus nigra*
Elder, Box	*Acer negundo*
	'Flamingo'
Elm	*Ulmus*
	'Columella'
	'New Horizons'
Elm, Wych	*Ulmus glabra*
	'Pendula'
False Acacia	*Robinia pseudoacacia*
Golden	*'Frisia'*
Fig	*Ficus carica*
Fir, Grand	*Abies grandis*
Flannelbush, Californian	*Fremontodendron californicum*
Foxglove Tree	*Paulownia tomentosa*
Ginkgo	*Ginkgo biloba*
Golden Rain Tree	*Koelreuteria paniculata*
	'Fastigiata'
Gorse	*Ulex europaeus*

Gum, Snow	*Eucalyptus pauciflora*
	ssp. niphophila
Handkerchief Tree	*Davidia involucrata*
Hawthorn	*Crataegus monogyna*
Hawthorn, Midland	*Crataegus laevigata*
	'Paul's Scarlet'
Hazel	*Corylus avelana*
Hazel, Turkish	*Corylus colurna*
Hibiscus	*Hibiscus syriaca*
Holly	*Ilex aquifolium*
Honey Locust	*Gleditsia tricathos*
Hornbeam	*Carpinus betulus*
	'Fastigiata'
Hornbeam, Hop	*Ostrya carpinifolia*
Hornbeam, Japanese	*Carpinus japonica*
Horse Chestnut	*Aesculus hippocastanum*
Horse Chestnut, Indian	*Aesculus indica*
Horse Chestnut, Red	*Aesculus x carnea*
Ironwood, Catalina	*Lyanothamnus*
	floribundus
Ironwood, Persian	*Parottia persica*
Judas Tree	*Cercis siliquastrum*
Juneberry	*Amelanchier lamarckii*
Juniper, Meyer's	*Juniperus squamata*
	'Meyeri'
Katsura	*Cercidiphyllum japonicum*
Kohuhu, 'Silver Queen'	*Pittosporum tenuifolium*
Lacebark, Long-leaved	*Hoheria sexstylosa*
Lancewood	*Pseudopanax crassifolius*
Lilac	*Syringa vulgaris*
Lime, Common	*Tilia x europaea*
Lime, Silver	*Tilia tomentosa*
	'Petiolaris'
Lime, Small-leaved	*Tilia cordata*
	'Winter Orange'
Loquat	*Eriobotrya japonica*
Magnolia	*Magnolia*
	'Heaven Scent'
	'Merrill'
Magnolia, Kobushi	*Magnolia kobus*
Magnolia, Saucer	*Magnolia x soulangeana*
Magnolia, Southern	*Magnolia grandiflora*
Maple, Cappadocian	*Acer cappadocicum*
Maple, Field	*Acer campestre*
Maple, Japanese	*Acer japonicum*
	'Atropurpurea'

Maple, Norway	*Acer platanoides*
Purple	*'Crimson King'*
	'Palmitifidum'
	'Drummondii'
	'Lorbergii'
Maple, Oregon	*Acer macrophyllum*
Maple, Paperbark	*Acer griseum*
Maple, Père David's	*Acer davidii*
Maple, Pheonix Snakebark	*Acer x conspicuum*
	'Phoenix'
Maple, Silver	*Acer saccharinum*
	'Wieri'
Maple, Sugar	*Acer saccharum*
Maple, Trident	*Acer buergerianum*
Medlar	*Mespilus germanica*
Mimosa	*Acacia dealbata*
Monkey Puzzle	*Araucaria araucana*
Moosewood	*Acer pennsylvanicum*
Mulberry, Black	*Morus nigra*
Mulberry, Paper	*Broussonetia papyrifera*
Mulberry, White	*Morus alba*
Weeping	*'Pendula'*
Myrtle, Crêpe	*Lagerstroemia indica*
Nettle Tree	*Celtis australis*
Oak, Holm	*Quercus ilex*
Oak, Hybrid	*Quercus x rosaceae*
Oak, Japanese Chestnut	*Quercus acutissima*
Oak, Pedunculate or English	
	Quercus robur
Oak, Cypress	*'Fastigiata Koster'*
Oak, Pin	*Quercus palustris*
Oak, Red	*Quercus rubra*
Oak, Scarlet	*Quercus coccinea*
Oak, Sessile	*Quercus petraea*
Oak, Spanish	*Quercus x hispanica*
Oak, Fulham	*'Fulhamensis'*
Oak, Lucombe	*'Lucombensis'*
Oak, Turkey	*Quercus cerris*
Olive	*Olea europaea*
Orange, Japanese Bitter	*Poncirus trifoliata*
Pagoda Tree, Japanese	*Styphnolobium*
	japonicum
Palm, Cabbage	*Cordyline australis*
Palm, Canary	*Phoenix canariensis*
Palm, Chusan	*Trachycarpus fortunei*
Peach, Hybrid	*Prunus x*

	amygdalo-persica
Peanut Butter Tree	*Clerodendrum trichotomum*
Pear	*Pyrus communis*
	'Beech Hill'
Pear, Chanticleer	*Pyrus calleryana 'Chanticleer'*
Pear, Willow-leaved	*Pyrus salicifolia*
Photinia, Red Robin	*Photinia fraseri 'Red Robin'*
Pine, Austrian	*Pinus nigra*
Pine, Scots	*Pinus sylvestris*
Pine, Stone	*Pinus pinea*
Pine, Wollemi	*Wollemia nobilis*
Plane, London	*Platanus x hispanica*
	'Pyramidalis'
	'Baobab'
	'Augustine Henry'
	'Palmata'
Plane, Oriental	*Platanus orientalis*
	'Digitata'
Poplar, Black	*Populus nigra ssp. betulifolia*
Poplar, Grey	*Populus canescens*
	'Tower'
Poplar, Hybrid Black	*Populus x canadensis*
Poplar, Lombardy	*Populus nigra 'Italica'*
Poplar, Plantière	*Populus nigra 'Plantierensis'*
Poplar, Variegated	*Populus x jackii 'Aurora'*
Poplar, White	*Populus alba*
Redwood, Coastal	*Sequoia sempervirens*
Redwood, Dawn	*Metasequoia glyptostroboides*
Redwood, Giant	*Sequoiadendron giganteum*
Rowan	*Sorbus aucuparia*
Rowan, Chinese Scarlet	*Sorbus commixta 'Embley'*
Sallow	*Salix cinerea ssp. oleifolia*
Service Tree of Fontainebleau	
	Sorbus latifolia
Service Tree, bastard	*Sorbus x thuringiaca*
Service Tree, True	*Sorbus domestica*
Service Tree, Wild	*Sorbus torminalis*
Silk Tree, Persian	*Albizia julibrissin*
'Soviet Tree'	*x Chitalpa tashkentensis*
Strawberry Tree	*Arbutus unedo*
Strawberry Tree, Hybrid	*Arbutus x andrachnoides*
Sweet Chestnut	*Castanea sativa*
Sweetgum, American	*Liquidambar styraciflua*
	'Silver King'
	'Slender Silhouette'
Sycamore	*Acer pseudoplatanus*
	'Spaethii'
Tamarisk, French	*Tamarix gallica*
Thorn, Broad-leaved Cockspur	
	Crataegus persimilis
	'Prunifolia'
Thorn, Scarlet	*Crataegus mollis*
Tree Fern	*Dicksonia antarctica*
Tree of Heaven	*Ailanthus altissima*
Tree Privet, Chinese	*Ligustrum lucidum*
	'Excelsum superbum'
Tulip Tree	*Liriodendron tulipifera*
	'Aureomarginata'
Tupelo	*Nyssa sylvatica*
Varnish Tree	*Toxicodendron vernicifluum*
Walnut, English	*Juglans regia*
Walnut, Manchurian	*Juglans mandshurica*
Wattle, Cootamundra	*Acacia baileyana*
Wedding Cake Tree	*Cornus controversa 'Variegatum'*
Whitebeam	*Sorbus aria*
	'Lutescens'
Whitebeam, Himalayan	*Sorbus vestita*
Whitebeam, Swedish	*Sorbus intermedia*
Willow, Corkscrew	*Salix babylonica var. pekinensis 'Torturosa'*
Willow, Crack	*Salix fragilis*
Willow, Goat	*Salix caprea*
Willow, Weeping	*Salix x sepulcralis*
Golden	*'Chrysocoma'*
Salamon's	*'Salamonii'*
Willow, White	*Salix alba*
Wingnut, Caucasian	*Pterocarya fraxinifolia*
Wisteria	*Wisteria sinensis*
Yew	*Taxus baccata*
Yew, Irish	*'Fastigiata'*
Zelkova, Japanese	*Zelkova serrata*

Index

Bibliography

Mark Blake, *Pigs Might Fly: The Inside Story of Pink Floyd* (Aurum, 2013)

Simon Bradley and Nikolaus Pevsner, *The Buildings of England, London 1: The City of London* (Yale, 2002)

John Boughton, *Municipal Dreams: The Rise and Fall of Council Housing* (Verso, 2018)

Bridget Cherry and Nikolaus Pevsner, *The Buildings of England, London 3: North West* (Yale, 2002)

Peter Coles, *Mulberry* (Reaktion Books, 2019)

R. S. R. Fitter, *London's Natural History* (Collins New Naturalist, 1945)

Ed Glinert, *The London Compendium* (Penguin, 2004)

Kirsty Hislop and Dominic Lutyens, *70s Style & Design* (Thames and Hudson, 2009)

Owen Johnson and David More, *Collins Tree Guide* (Collins, 2006)

Mark Johnston, *Trees in Towns and Cities: A History of British Arboriculture* (Windgather Press, 2015)

Mark Johnston, *Street Trees in Britain: A History* (Windgather Press, 2017)

Henry W. Lawrence, *City Trees: A Historical Geography from the Renaissance through the Nineteenth Century* (University of Virginia Press, 2006)

Rozelle Raynes, *Limehouse Lil* (Castweazel Publishing, 2006)

Michael Rosenberg, *Rebel Footprints: A Guide to Uncovering London's Radical History* (Pluto Press, 2019)

David Solman, *Loddiges of Hackney: The Largest Hothouse in the World* (Hackney Society, 1995)

Paul Talling, *London's Lost Rock Venues* (Damaged Goods, 2020)

Graham Taylor, *Ada Salter: Pioneer of Ethical Socialism* (Lawrence and Wishart, 2016)

Simon Wells, *She's a Rainbow: The Extraordinary Life of Anita Pallenberg* (Omnibus Press, 2020)

Discography

Original record labels are cited, which are not necessarily those of the current CD edition

Dr Feelgood, *Down by the Jetty* (United Artists)

Ian Dury, *New Boots and Panties* (Stiff)

Bob Marley and the Wailers, *Exodus* (Island)

Graham Parker and the Rumour, *Howlin' Wind* (Mercury)

Pink Floyd, *Echoes: The Very Best of* (Harvest)

Rolling Stones, *Singles Collection: The London Years* (London)

T. Rex, *Electric Warrior* (Fly)

The Who, *My Generation: The Very Best of* (Track)